FREDERICK & ANNA DOUGLASS IN ROCHESTER NEW YORK

FREDERICK & ANNA DOUGLASS

IN

ROCHESTER NEW YORK

> THEIR HOME WAS OPEN TO ALL

• ROSE O'KEEFE •

Charleston — London

THE
History
PRESS

Published by The History Press
Charleston, SC 29403
www.historypress.net

Cover image: Frederick Douglass. *Library of Congress.*

First published 2013

Manufactured in the United States

ISBN 978.1.62619.181.5

Library of Congress CIP data applied for.

I consider the authors whose works I read for this project to be true friends. All have their own slants and contributions to understanding a fuller picture—in particular, Dickson J. Preston in Young Frederick Douglass; *Peter Burchard in* Frederick Douglass: For the Great Family of Man; *and* The Frederick Douglass Papers *series, edited by John Blassingame, John McKivigan and Peter Hanks. Thank you to all of them and to their many helpers behind the scenes.*

Contents

Acknowledgements

This book could not have been written without the help of services and individuals, including:

- Rochester Public Library, especially the Local History Division at the downtown public library
- Curator Lea Kemp at the Rochester Museum and Science Center
- Local history authors Ruth Rosenberg-Naparsteck and Emerson Klees
- Curator Kamil McClarin at the Frederick Douglass National Park
- Whistle Stop Writers group
- Consultant Lonna Cosmano
- Curator Bill Keeler at the Rochester Historical Society

Very special thanks go to retired University of Rochester archivist Karl Kabelac for his invaluable support.

Introduction

*F*rederick and Anna Douglass in Rochester, New York shares the personal side of one of the most famous public and political men of the 1800s: Frederick Douglass. My quest to uncover more about his family began about ten years ago, when a man sitting in the local history section of the downtown Rochester Public Library noticed what I was reading—any one of the noncirculating Douglass biographies. He told me that some of the Douglass children had attended 13 School on Gregory Street in Rochester (which happens to be my neighborhood).

That comment started my search to learn everything I could about the Douglass family. Although researchers have devoted decades to cataloguing five thousand pieces of his public writings, speeches and travels in the marvelous series "The Frederick Douglass Papers," details about the family are much harder to come by. Personal tidbits were shared only with close friends.

In his first autobiography, *Narrative of the Life of Frederick Douglass*, Douglass wrote about the harshness of slave life and how he came to flee to New York City. I am grateful that his early years in Maryland have been well described by Dickson J. Preston in *Young Frederick Douglass* and Peter Burchard in *Frederick Douglass: For the Great Family of Man*. Douglass retells his story more accurately in his second autobiography, *My Bondage and My Freedom*, which describes his early years up to fleeing to New York City and moving to New Bedford, Massachusetts.

Both autobiographies and biographies give a clear view of his early years but much less of the decades when Frederick and Anna's children were young.

This book aims to fill in the gaps in their family history with information and vintage images of their twenty-five years in Rochester, New York.

Despite living through one of our nation's most bitter and terrifying times, Frederick and Anna raised five children in loving homes with flower, fruit and vegetable gardens. Their house was open to fugitives, visitors and houseguests who stayed for weeks, months and years at a time. Their grown children moved back into their parents' house when jobs were scarce both in Rochester and later in Washington, D.C. All of these comings and goings went on while Anna, whose health was weak after five children, stayed home and Frederick traveled.

I gleaned details about the family's life from several biographies, scholarly endnotes in the autobiographies and correspondence series and family letters, as well as from what their daughter, Rosetta Douglass Sprague, wrote in the early 1900s. She said that her father's story had already been well told, but her mother's had not. All have contributed to this portrait of the Douglass family and how they came to call Rochester, New York, their home for twenty-five years.

Chapter 1

Tuckahoe, Maryland, to New York City

After slavery was abolished in Maryland in November 1864, Frederick Douglass returned to Fells Point in Baltimore for the first time since 1838, when, at age twenty, he had escaped from that city. In the years since he fled, he had traveled widely in the United States and the British Isles, but it is unlikely he could have foreseen living in Rochester, New York—let alone for twenty-five years. He always remained a Marylander and a proud Eastern Shoreman at heart but came to call Rochester his home and chose to be buried there.

Narrative of the Life of Frederick Douglass, An American Slave, Written by Himself, his first autobiography, begins simply: "I was born in Tuckahoe, near Hillsborough, and about twelve miles from Easton, in Talbot county, Maryland. I have no accurate knowledge of my age, never having seen any authentic record containing it." Frederick's birth name was Frederick Augustus Washington Bailey, and he was called Freddy Bailey.

In his second book, *My Bondage and My Freedom,* Douglass described Tuckahoe as a drab and dreary neighborhood, surrounded by poor whites. He guessed at the origin of the name Tuckahoe without knowing it came from the Algonquin word for root or mushroom.

He said his mother, Harriet Bailey, the daughter of Isaac and Betsey Bailey, was darker in color than either of her parents. That his father was white was common knowledge; that his father was his master, Aaron Anthony, or "Captain Anthony," was hinted at. Since he and his mother had little time together, he barely knew or remembered her.

HISTORICAL MARKER

*Frederick Douglass Abolitionist/
Orator/Author
Frederick Douglass was born into
American slavery on Maryland's
Eastern Shore in February 1818.
In March 1826, Douglass, a slave
child, was sent to live in the Hugh
Auld household at this location, from
1826–1831.*

HISTORICAL MARKERS

*Douglass periodically resided in
Fells Point as a slave until Monday,
September 3, 1838, when he escaped to
freedom via the Underground Railroad.
Douglass returned to Baltimore as a
free man on May 19, 1870 to address
the 20,000 participants in the 15th
Amendment Celebration and Parade*

*Frederick Douglass, one of
America's greatest freedom fighters,
died in Washington, DC on February
20, 1895. He was buried in
Rochester, NY.*

(Both of these markers are located
at the intersection of Aliceanna
Street and South Durham Street,
Baltimore, Maryland)

"Aunt Betsey," as his grandmother was called, raised dozens of children whose mothers labored in distant fields. Despite living in an old windowless log cabin with a clay floor and dirt chimney, the cabin was a haven for children like Freddy. Aunt Betsey delighted in having the children, mostly of her own daughters, around her. The daughters were Jenny, Esther, Milly, Priscilla and Harriet. For much of the first seven years of his life, Freddy wore only a long shirt and had no possessions. Even so, if he stayed away from tough older boys, he was as happy as could be.

Freddy's carefree days ended on a summer morning when he and Aunt Bestey left the swampy backwoods for a brick house on the Lloyd Plantation, where his master lived with his daughter Lucretia and her husband, Thomas Auld.

After they had walked for several hours and arrived at the plantation, Aunt Betsey encouraged him to play with his brother Perry, sisters Sarah and Eliza and several cousins. When Freddy realized his grandmother was gone, he collapsed, crying because she had left without warning. His two years there—where he was called in local dialect "Captain Anthony Fed"— were painful for being underfed and witnessing brutal beatings. The most common reason for whippings was oversleeping.

Lucretia Auld, who was fond of him, most likely encouraged her father to send Freddy to Baltimore to live with her brother-in-law, Hugh Auld, to care for Hugh's young son. So in the spring of 1826, Freddy traveled on a sloop, along with six hundred sheep headed for slaughter. On the way, he had his first sighting ever of a city—Annapolis—plus the excitement of unloading the sheep and walking to his home in a shipbuilding neighborhood. But

HISTORICAL MARKER

A colonial maritime community established 1726 by William Fell, shipbuilder of Lancashire, England. In this area were built more than six hundred ships from the colonial era through the Civil War. Birthplace of the U.S. Frigate "Constellation" and home port of the famous Baltimore clippers.

(Located at the intersection of Thames Street and Broadway, Baltimore, Maryland)

the greeting he received at the door of the Auld house stunned him. Sophia Auld beamed at him with delight and greeted him like her own boy, Tommy. For the first time ever, Freddy had worn pants and a shirt on the sloop. That night in the Aulds' home, he sat at their table with them, ate their food and then slept in a loft on a straw mattress with a sheet and blanket.

This sweet time didn't last. First Hugh Auld became outraged at his wife's mistake of teaching the alphabet to Freddy alongside Tommy. Then Freddy's master, Aaron Anthony, died in November 1826, and as a piece of property, Freddy had to return to the Lloyd Plantation for the settlement of the will. Sophia burst into tears when Freddy left for the plantation, where he was threatened by one of his potential masters.

Despite the initial scare of where he would eventually go, Freddy was sent back and stayed seven years at Hugh and Sophia Auld's home, where he taught himself to read and write in secret. When he was twelve, he learned the meaning of the word "abolition" in a newspaper and bought himself a copy of the inspirational *Columbian Orator*. Around age thirteen, he had a religious conversion.

Stress in the Auld household grew after Sophia had two more children, and Hugh drank more as his business failed. Even though Freddy and Sophia had grown apart, what finally separated them was Thomas Auld's resentment at owning Henny, a crippled slave, while his brother Hugh had the advantage of

This view of Federal Hill in Baltimore, Maryland (circa 1831), shows the port area around the time Frederick Bailey lived there. *Library of Congress.*

Freddy's able services. Thomas said that if Hugh had Freddy, then he should also have Henny, and he sent her to Baltimore. Hugh sent her back, and Thomas, as owner of both, demanded that Hugh return Freddy.

In March 1833, Freddy returned to Thomas Auld's household of eight in the rundown shipbuilding village of St. Michael's. After his wife Lucretia's death, Thomas had married a sickly woman who was stingy and cruel about feeding their slaves. The Aulds lived in the house behind Thomas's store, while Freddy, his younger sister Eliza and their Aunt Priscilla and cousin Henny lived in a kitchen building. Freddy, now fifteen, was constantly hungry. Eliza taught him that the sin of stealing food did not apply to slaves.

In January 1834, he was serviced out to work for a year on Edward Covey's farm, where Freddy slept in an unheated attic and shivered through many cold nights. Covey was a hardworking, bullish, churchgoing farmer who whipped or beat Freddy weekly. That August, when Freddy swooned on a sweltering day, Covey struck him to force him to get back to work, but instead Freddy ran to Thomas Auld for protection—which Auld refused to give. A few days later, Covey tried to tie him up for a beating, but Freddy fought back. After a long and vicious struggle, Covey told Freddy to get back to work and never lashed him again.

When Freddy returned to Thomas Auld's home on Christmas Day, he saw how the tradition of slaves binge-drinking until the New Year kept them in place. On the first of January 1835, he was hired out for the year on

William Freeland's farm. This non-religious master gave them enough food, time to eat it and work hours from sunrise to sunset. It was there that Freddy assisted with a Sabbath school, where up to forty students met to learn the Bible on Sunday—a time he remembered with great fondness.

Then, when Freddy was rehired for another year's service at the Freeland farm, his determination to live *freely* grew. After a failed escape plan, he was sent back to Hugh Auld, who apprenticed him as a caulker in a shipyard, where instead he ran errands for seventy-five carpenters working on two warships. This frustrating arrangement ended when four white apprentices beat him so badly that he almost lost his left eye.

Unlike Thomas Auld, who had agreed with Covey's beatings, Hugh Auld stood up for him—without success—in the local courts. Then, and as foreman in another yard, Hugh hired Freddy as caulking apprentice. Within a year, Freddy was able to hire out at the highest wage for experienced caulkers and found that the more freedom he had, the more discontented he felt.

From that time on, Freddy set his mind on escaping. In May 1838, he persuaded Hugh Auld to let him move out while committing to pay Hugh weekly, no matter how much work he had. By August, Freddy had stretched his privileges and lost the agreement. He then set September 3 as the day he would flee. In the *Narratives*, he glosses over the details in order to protect those who aided him.

After a nerve-wracking escape by train and ferry, he arrived in New York City, exhausted, and survived alone and hungry before finding David Ruggles, who took him in. Ruggles, a black activist in the antislavery cause, helped him decide to find work as a caulker in New Bedford. Freddy wrote to Anna Murray, a house servant who had helped him escape. She joined him in New York, where they were married by the Reverend James W.C. Pennington on September 15. He had changed his name to Frederick Johnson, but Douglass did not reveal these details publicly until 1881.

FREDERICK BAILEY JOHNSON married a strong woman much like his mother, Harriet Bailey, and grandmother, Betsey Bailey. All the women he was close to as an adult had the same strength, independence and devotion. He was not attracted to the Victorian model of a submissive child wife. White women with whom he later worked closely included Julia Griffiths, Ottilie Assing and Helen Pitts, who gave him the education and middle-class social skills that few black women would have been able to share and that he wanted.

Chapter 2

New Bedford, Massachusetts, to Rochester, New York

LIFE IN NEW BEDFORD

Frederick and Anna Johnson took the train from New York City to New Bedford, Massachusetts, where they stayed with Mary and Nathan Johnson in a house on Seventh Street that had once been the Friends' meetinghouse and where Mary ran a popular confectionery shop. Nathan, the only African American member of the local library society, suggested Frederick choose a different surname, taking a heroic name from literature. Without needing to look at Sir Walter Scott's popular poem "Lady on the Lake," Frederick chose Douglass, spelling it the way prominent black families in Baltimore and Philadelphia did.

In *Bondage and Freedom*, he described how the shock of not being able to earn good wages as a skilled caulker because of local racism was offset by the joy of keeping every penny he earned in any way he could for the next three years.

Frederick borrowed a saw from Nathan and found work with saw, buck (sawhorse) and axe chopping wood. He hauled heavy fittings, shoveled coal, dug cellars, cleared rubbish, worked on the wharves, loaded and unloaded vessels and scoured cabins. Anna was pregnant. In the spring, he found work with set wages moving casks of whale oil—hard work that required the kind of strength Douglass was proud to have.

A few months after their arrival in New Bedford, he was introduced to the abolitionist newspaper the *Liberator*, and even though he couldn't afford it, he somehow became a subscriber to the weekly paper, which soon "took its place with me next to the bible." For three years, he learned as much as he could about the antislavery cause.

Frederick and Anna settled into their new life in New Bedford. After attending a mostly white Methodist church, he switched to Zion Chapel, an African Methodist Episcopal Zion denomination, where Bishop Christopher Rush gave him authority to act as an exhorter. Frederick said the days he spent in little Zion as sexton, steward, class leader, clerk and local preacher were among the happiest days of his life.

In March 1839, Frederick had spoken up cautiously at a church meeting about what slavery was like and why slaves should be freed. Reading a notice about his words in William Lloyd Garrison's *Liberator* gave him his first taste of public attention. Shortly afterward, Reverend James noticed him in the audience where he was speaking and invited Frederick to share his story. This time, Frederick spoke about his own life.

When Frederick heard Garrison speak for the first time in April 1839, he heard a strong and passionate voice he never forgot. Although he felt inspired by the Reverend James, Frederick couldn't blend religion with his antislavery zeal and chose the secular Garrison as his mentor.

It was at Zion that he met a remarkable new preacher: the Reverend Thomas James, who had been ordained in 1833 by Bishop Rush and had merged his religious zeal with his drive to end slavery. Reverend James licensed Frederick to preach as a lay preacher.

By 1841, the Douglass family was settled in New Bedford. They had moved from their small house into a larger house on Ray Street, where Anna had her garden and where, in the evenings, Frederick played Haydn, Mozart and Handel on his violin. Their lifestyle was close to the middle-class life Anna would have known in Baltimore. They were expecting a third child.

Gradually, Frederick's speaking circle grew larger, and he spoke in August 1841 at the Massachusetts Anti-slavery Convention in Nantucket. For two hours, he let loose before a packed audience with a riveting account of his life. This first great public speech was enhanced by

---

HISTORICAL MARKER

Frederick Douglass 1818–1895.
"For my part, I should prefer death to hopeless bondage."
New Bedford 1838–1841.

(Near 133 William Street in New Bedford, Massachusetts)

Garrison's passionate call afterward: "Shall such a man be held a slave in a Christian land?" to which the audience of Quakers shouted, "No! No!"

Afterward, Frederick was invited to tour as a speaker for the Anti-slavery Society. That fall, the family moved to a cottage in Lynn, Massachusetts, that the society helped them buy. Lynn was described as a pleasant town with "sweeping views of the distant shipping lanes." Most of the residents were white, and many were liberal.

Douglass wasn't home much because he often took the train into Boston. With help from friends, he bought a horse and buggy for Anna and also sent her money. She managed the household, raised the children and, as she had done in Baltimore, worked as a domestic.

Frederick and Anna's first four children were born in Massachusetts. Rosetta was born in their two-room home on Elm Street overlooking Buzzard's Bay on June 24, 1839; Lewis Henry was born on July 10, 1840, in New Bedford; Frederick Jr. on March 3, 1842; and Charles on October 21, 1844, "in a nice little cottage" in Lynn.

THE FIRST AUTOBIOGRAPHY

Even though Frederick Douglass was becoming an acclaimed national speaker, people still doubted that anyone who spoke so well could ever have been a slave. To prove them wrong, during the winter of 1844–45 he decided to write down the story of his youth and publish it—without giving his former name or the names of those who had helped him flee. He shared his life story publicly at the annual meeting of the American Anti-Slavery Society in New York City in May 1845 and published the book at the end of the month. The book's publication was a bold move that threatened his freedom.

Five thousand copies of *Narrative of the Life of Frederick Douglass, An American Slave, Written by Himself*, were released by the Anti-Slavery Office in Boston and sold for fifty cents each. By the fall, 4,500 copies were sold in the United States, and soon there were three European editions.

Because of strong ties between the abolitionists in the United States and Great Britain, Maria Weston Chapman, William Lloyd Garrison and Wendell Phillips, of the Anti-Slavery Society in Boston, decided it was more important to have him speak abroad than at home. *Narrative* included a preface by Frederick's famous mentor, William Lloyd Garrison.

Below is a reproduction of a reprint from "The Silver Standard," published in 1847, and showing a quaint old woodcut of Mr. Douglass, with information concerning him. "The Silver Standard" is the publication of the Rogers Bros. silverware company. Recently it has reprinted its old back numbers.

THE SILVER STANDARD, DECEMBER, 1847.

FRED DOUGLASS.

THE negro orator, Frederick Douglass, has located in Rochester, N. Y., and has started a paper, which, we understand, is to be devoted to the anti-slavery principle. This former slave has made quite a name for himself by his efforts in behalf of his own race and may make considerable of a stir before many years.

A rare newspaper print of Frederick Douglass in 1847. *Rochester Historical Society.*

In those days, autobiographies were considered a higher form of literature than fiction, and *Narrative* was the most widely reviewed black autobiography before the Civil War. It was praised in newspapers and magazines in the United States, British Isles and Europe.

Not all reviews were flattering. Slaveholders in Talbot County, Maryland, were furious. One man who had known Freddy Bailey during the time he worked under Edward Covey considered him nothing but a lowly slave and staunchly defended the character of Colonel Lloyd, Thomas Auld and others.

TRAVEL ABROAD

Although Frederick Douglass seldom mentions it in his letters, he sailed on a steam packet called the *Cambria* from Boston to England on August 16, 1845, with James Buffam, whom the Boston Anti-slavery Society leaders had chosen as his traveling companion.

Buffam, who was a successful carpenter from Lynn, was described as a pleasant and mild-mannered man, a loyal friend and abolitionist. He had booked a double room in first class, but the shipping agent wouldn't allow a black man to travel with whites, so they both slept in a modest room in steerage and considered the downgrade a thrifty move. Not only did Buffum smooth the bumps along the way, but he also handled the money.

Except for the first-class stateroom, Frederick was free to come and go on the rest of the ship and took long walks alone on the upper decks. If the seas were too rough, he and Buffam relaxed in the second-class saloon with the Hutchinson Family Singers and others.

Judson, John Wallace, Asa and Abigail Jemina Hutchinson were four of thirteen of Polly and Jesse Hutchinson's children who performed as a musical quartet. They had performed in Lynn, where Frederick had inspired them to join the movement. After traveling across with them, Douglass went to Dublin, where they later met up with him to perform at meetings.

The Hutchinson Family Singers were a famous quartet that sang about rural life as well as abolition, temperance, politics, war and women's suffrage.

On the last day of the crossing, the shipmaster invited Frederick to talk informally about slavery on the second deck. The scene that followed was written up in the English papers. A sympathizer wrote that drunken American slaveholders heckled him and then threatened to throw him overboard. The captain quickly intervened, and the news of Douglass's safe arrival spread quickly.

After the *Cambria* docked in the port of Liverpool on August 28, Douglass, Buffum and the Hutchinson singers stayed in a hotel for two days without

The Hutchinson Family Singers were from Milford, New Hampshire, and traveled with Douglass to the British Isles. *Library of Congress.*

incident. Then the *Cambria* sailed across the Irish Sea to Dublin, where Frederick was to begin his tour.

In his first talk in a prosperous town, Frederick saw a carpet mill that matched comparable mills in New Bedford, but local wealth and opulence surpassed Wye House on the Lloyd Plantation.

Among the first people Frederick met was Richard D. Webb, a Dublin Quaker, a founder of the Hibernian Antislavery Society and publisher of antislavery books. Webb, who published the *Narrative* in 1845 and 1846, knew William Lloyd Garrison and also arranged speaking tours for abolitionists in Ireland. His brother Thomas was a bookseller and printer in Dublin. Richard's wife, Hannah W. Webb, was also a strong figure in the Irish antislavery movement, edited the *Anti-Slavery Advocate* with him and corresponded with many women's rights advocates.

Through arrangements made by Maria Chapman, secretary of the Antislavery Society in Boston, Douglass and Buffum were to stay with the Webbs while Frederick worked out the details of Richard's publishing and marketing of the *Narrative*. Webb went on to print five editions of the *Narrative*, selling five hundred copies by November 1845.

Next, Frederick stayed for a month with the Jennings—a large family who belonged to the Church of Ireland—who were at ease with their neighbors, despite being surrounded by Roman Catholics. He relaxed and enjoyed the music, talks and chatter among the parents and their three sons and five daughters.

Frederick Douglass quickly became an advocate for temperance. He wrote to Garrison that he and James Buffum attended a festive evening of 250 temperance supporters hosted by Father Theobald Mathew, an enormously popular temperance leader. Frederick wrote that no one was put off by his color, unlike at similar gatherings in New England. After his bad experiences with drinking as a young slave, he readily took the pledge.

From Dublin, Frederick Douglass went to England, where he and James Buffum began an intense lecture tour in Manchester—England's largest textile city—whose many looms ran on cotton grown by slaves in the southern United States.

Both in Manchester and in the large industrial city of Birmingham, Frederick saw workers rallying for a living wage. Their miserable working conditions and the crushing poverty of countless beggars in the streets and countryside impressed on him the common needs of all workers. His commitment to the rights and dignity of all of humanity was forged during these travels.

Although he never mentioned it publicly, Frederick Douglass could not help but notice the devastation caused by the potato famine, which started with a crop failure in 1845, then a blight and complete crop failure in 1846. (Famine and malnutrition caused two million deaths between 1841 and 1851 because 75 percent of the Irish lived off homegrown food.)

The news from October 1845 that Thomas Auld had sold Frederick Bailey to his brother Hugh for $100 did not reach him for several months.

In early January 1846, Frederick gave his last major speech in Ireland at a public breakfast sponsored by the Belfast Anti-slavery Society before sailing to Glasgow to start his tour of Scotland.

After all two thousand copies were sold by March 1846, Webb printed a second edition in February 1846. About thirteen thousand copies of the *Narrative* sold in Ireland and England between 1845 and 1847.

TRAVEL IN SCOTLAND

Before Frederick Douglass started on the tour of Scotland in 1846, there were growing strains between him and the New England abolitionists who treated him like a celebrity fugitive who needed watching over rather than a peer. William Lloyd Garrison thought it might be best for Douglass to go home to his wife and children, but Frederick, who often gave three speeches a day, wasn't about to slow down.

Starting in January, Frederick Douglass teamed up with James Buffum, Henry Wright and George Thompson to tackle the controversial topic of the large contributions that the Free Church of Scotland received from slaveholders in the American South.

After "a proud week for our cause" in Glasgow, they continued to speak across Scotland, and as Frederick's fame soared, he grew cocky over his phenomenal success. He wrote to Francis Jackson, the wealthy president of the Massachusetts Anti-slavery Society, that he was being treated as an equal and a brother wherever he went, the same way Jackson had treated him the first time they met in Nantucket.

Ironically, because some abolitionists wished he were "blacker," to avoid crediting his success to his whiteness, Douglass let his wooly hair grow out in order "to pass for at least half a negro."

While in Scotland, word finally reached Douglass that Thomas Auld had transferred his title of ownership to his brother Hugh. The abolitionist press didn't hesitate to spread the threat that Hugh intended to return him to "the cotton fields of the South" if Frederick ever came back. That remark was never confirmed as more than idle talk, but the report that Thomas gave him to Hugh as a gift was false.

THE BILL OF SALE was filed in Talbot County, Maryland, on November 30, 1846, and a formal deed of manumission was registered in the Baltimore County courthouse on December 12, 1846. Those who helped Frederick also included U.S. Quakers Lindley Murray Moore and Isaac and Amy Post, and he received his manumission papers on December 5, 1846.

Douglass had to make a decision. In the time since the *Narrative* had been printed, it had been read by almost one million people on both sides of the Atlantic, making him a thorn in the sides of American slaveholders. Knowing there were some who would execute him in public as a lesson to their slaves, he accepted the offer from English supporters to pay Hugh Auld for his freedom. This decision caused some New England abolitionists to criticize him for allowing the purchase of freedom to validate the legality of slavery.

Perhaps out of jealousy or curiosity, William Lloyd Garrison decided to join the speaking tour that summer. Before then, Douglass spoke in London many times, where he was, again, very popular. He spoke for up to three hours at a time on the effects of slavery on slaves, as well as on the U.S. Congress, which had ruled that each slave be counted as three-fifths of a man to increase their numbers in the House of Representatives.

He horrified audiences with stories about how "the whip, the chain, the gag, the thumbscrew, the blood-hound, the stocks" rebutted the lie that slaves were happy. After one of his impassioned speeches, the chairman of the group said, "There is not a foot of ground in the United States where Frederick Douglass's legal owner would not have a right to seize him!"

While visiting with Ellen Richardson and her brother and sister-in-law, Henry and Anna Richardson, in Newcastle upon Tyne in July, Ellen and Henry took him to the seashore. Ellen, the headmistress of a girls' school and abolitionist, noticed his painful struggle with bringing his wife and family over and decided to work on buying his freedom.

Douglass wrote to Garrison that he missed his family, friends and work very much but had no intention of living in Britain, except to protect his freedom.

DURING HIS ABSENCE

Frederick arranged for Anna and the children to receive the proceeds from the book sales during his absence. From 1846 to 1848, their oldest child, Rosetta, stayed with Abigail and Lydia Mott and attended school in Albany. Rosetta stayed with the Mott sisters, who were very fond of her, while the three boys, Lewis Henry, five; Frederick Jr., three; and Charles Remond, one (in 1845) stayed with Anna in Lynn.

Anna was a core member of the Lynn and Boston Anti-slavery Societies, and each woman in the Lynn society helped her with chores on the morning of the sewing circle. Anna also earned money by binding shoes, donated a portion of her earnings to the society and put aside a portion for a rainy day. Anna was a skilled domestic worker who did not read or write well, so during her childhood, Rosetta wrote for and read letters to her. Rosetta also helped with housework and the piecework that Anna did for the shoe factories in Lynn.

Frederick sent her money as he was able, and after he returned, she showed him all the money, both his and hers, that she had set aside without having taken on any debts while he was gone. She felt supported and comforted by her friends in Massachusetts.

Frederick Douglass traveled homeward on the *Cambria* on April 4, 1847, from Liverpool, England, arriving in Halifax on April 18 and Boston on April 20. In a letter dated April 3, he complained of having purchased a ticket for passage on the *Cambria* with the assurance of enjoying the same rights and privileges as other passengers. To his dismay, upon boarding the steamer in the company of friends, he learned his berth had been sold and the company agent had no authority to sell him that ticket.

He made a detour to the company offices, only to be told that he could not board the ship without agreeing to take his meals alone, not mingle with the other passengers and give up his berth. He wrote that after traveling nineteen months enjoying equal rights and privileges wherever he went throughout the British Isles, it wasn't until he turned his "face towards America" that he met such discrimination.

When he finally arrived in Lynn, Douglass rushed from the train and met Lewis and Frederick, two bright-eyed boys, "running and dancing with joy to meet me. Taking one in my arms and the other by the hand, I hastened to my house." He then attended welcoming receptions in Lynn on April 23, in Boston on May 3, in New Bedford on May 23 and in New York City on May 26.

FREDERICK RETURNED TO the United States a changed man. He had seen the harsh working conditions in coal mines and factories in Great Britain, as well as the horrors of the potato famine, and was more determined than ever to stand up for the rights of blacks. Abolitionist friends in the United States were not convinced his paper could withstand competition from other abolitionist papers.

In a letter to Anna Richardson, he mentioned the "foretaste of what now awaits me in this boasted land of republican freedom." Then he told how Anna, who was in much better health than he had expected to find her, was "exceedingly happy to have me once more at home." He described the joy he had in meeting his boys at the station in Lynn and said that he and Anna planned to see Rosetta shortly. In early May, they visited their daughter in Albany.

Relations between Frederick Douglass and William Lloyd Garrison were strained at times, but Douglass and Garrison traveled agreeably in Pennsylvania and Ohio that summer. Before they parted in the fall, Douglass had not mentioned his plan to start his own paper to Garrison, but the hostility they experienced while on tour convinced Frederick that his newspaper was needed.

After his decision to become a newspaper editor led to his being fired as a lecturer by the Anti-Slavery Society, Douglass said, "I shall be under no party or society, but shall advocate the slave's cause in the way which in my judgment will be best suited to the advancement of the cause." His declaration of independence was his claim to manhood and personal freedom from a role imposed and defined by those who called themselves his friends and yet considered his independence to be ingratitude.

A NEW HOME

In late October 1847, Frederick Douglass wrote a note to abolitionist Amy Post that he planned to make Rochester his home and was buying the supplies he needed to publish the first issues of his paper in mid-November. In the 1840s, the Rochester region matched New England in its zeal to end slavery. It was conveniently located along the Erie Canal and railroads, mid-way between New England and the Midwest for his lecture tours.

The AME Zion Church was built in Rochester on Spring and Favor Streets in 1835. The first issue of the *North Star* was printed in its basement. *Rochester Images, Rochester Public Library Local History Division.*

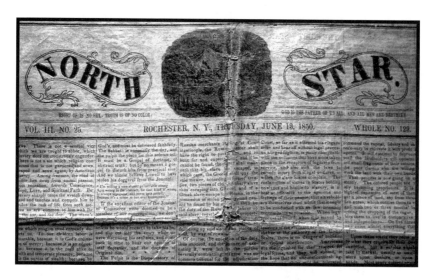

The first issue of the *North Star* was printed and distributed in December 1847.
Rochester Images, Rochester Public Library Local History Division.

The Reynolds Arcade on Buffalo Street was a successful commercial building across
the street from where Frederick Douglass worked as editor of the *North Star*. *Rochester
Images, Rochester Public Library Local History Division.*

On November 1, Frederick Douglass wrote from Lynn, Massachusetts, to Jonathan D. Carr, son of a Quaker grocer who worked as a baker in Carlisle, England, thanking him for his generous gift of "two thousand, one hundred, and seventy-five dollars." He informed his dear friend that "it is already, appropriated to the very purpose originally intended, both my myself and the donors—the establishment of a press to advocate the cause of the American slave, and to elevate and improve the condition of the nominally-free coloured people in the United States."

In early December, Frederick wrote at great length to politician and slave owner Henry Clay, whose sensational speech against the controversial annexation of the Mexican territories had been reprinted in newspapers across the country. Douglass wrote, "My position under this government, even in the State of N.Y., is that of a disenfranchised man...I approach you simply in the character of one of the unhappy millions enduring the evils of Slavery, in this otherwise highly favored and glorious land."

Douglass was referring to a change in the New York State Constitution in 1821 that had removed property requirements for white men but required black men to be residents of the state for three years and have over $250 in real property before they could vote. Since he had only recently moved to the state, and lacked any real property, Douglass couldn't vote. He

ALTHOUGH BLACK ABOLITIONIST and clergyman Samuel R. Ward claimed racial prejudice was less active and less bitter in western New York than in other parts of the country, he considered the region the very battle ground of impartial freedom because African Americans were expected to achieve more there than in places where they were overlooked, neglected and despised. The women of Upstate New York also contributed to the antislavery effort while challenging the gender-based restrictions of the antebellum decades.

The Rochester Ladies' Antislavery Society conformed to local codes of racial and sexual conduct, rejected demands for women's rights and maintained respectability in public and in private; women in the Western New York Antislavery Society wore bloomers, discussed the sexual brutality of slavery, demanded sexual equality and socialized in mixed-race company—to the dismay of their neighbors.

included his entire letter to Henry Clay in the first issue of the *North Star* on December 3, 1847.

Philanthropist Gerrit Smith wrote in the beginning of December from Peterboro, New York, sending Frederick Douglass a draft for five dollars for a two-year subscription to the paper. He also sent deeds to two parcels of land for Douglass and William C. Nell, one of the original editors of the paper, now that they were both residents of the state and would own property.

That year, Smith had donated 140,000 acres of land in Franklin and Essex Counties to three thousand black citizens of New York State. The climate was "rigorous," and the farmland was of poor quality, but the deeds gave many a chance to become independent.

A BEACON LIGHT

On January 1, 1848, David Ruggles, the free black man who had helped Douglass in 1838 in New York City and ran a printing and book shop that focused on abolition, wrote to Frederick Douglass:

> *Dear Friends Douglass and Delaney: The specimen number of the* North Star, *is just what it should be—a beacon light of liberty, to illuminate the pathway of the bleeding, hunted fugitive of the South; and to arouse our disenfranchised fellow-countrymen and women of the North, who are lulled to sleep by the syren song of Liberty, while we are* slaves *to all intents, purposes, and constructions, in any state within this SLAVEHOLDING UNION.*

Abolitionist William Nell wrote in 1848 that the *Car of Freedom* had forwarded to Canada nearly twenty thousand slaves. Sorting fact from fiction about the volume of traffic on the highway to heaven is a difficult task. What is clear is that Upstate New York was a major escape route.

In a letter to Amy Post from Albany at the end of January, Frederick told her he was lecturing that evening at the courthouse in Troy. He added, "I found my Dear Rosetta quite well and delighted to see her father."

Abolitionist minister Jermain Wesley Loguen wrote to Frederick Douglass from Syracuse in early February: "I am myself a fugitive from the land of whips and chains; and might never have made my escape had there been no North Star…I welcome your labors as an editor, and long to do all I can 'to strengthen your hands and encourage your heart.'"

Douglas wrote to Amy Post's husband, Isaac, from Lynn in February 1848 that he would be bringing his family from Lynn to Rochester in about a week. He asked Isaac to find him a place to rent costing not more than "one hundred dollars per annum." He had spoken in Richfield, Troy and Springfield on the way to Lynn and was kept busy getting subscribers to the paper. Frederick mentioned visiting "Friend Garrison…[who] was well and made affectionate enquires for the health of your family."

When they moved into their house on Alexander Street near East Avenue, Frederick and Anna's children were: Rosetta, eight; Lewis, seven; Frederick Jr., five; and Charles, three. Their neighbors were abolitionists on one side and Adventist prophet William Miller on the other. When he was home, his neighbors enjoyed listening to Frederick play his favorite songs on the violin, including, "Nelly was a Lady" and "Old Kentucky Home." He also sang, in a rich baritone, songs like "Carry Me Back to Ole Virginny."

ISAAC POST, A DRUGGIST, and his wife, Amy, who helped persuade Frederick to move upstate, helped many refugees at their Plymouth Avenue home. Amy Post estimated that 150 refugees passed through Rochester each year.

Because of his wide fame, Frederick Douglass became the chief local agent of the Underground Railroad and, with a dozen confederates, assisted four hundred freedom-seeking fugitives reach Canada. He worked closely with Harriet Tubman, Isaac and Amy Post, the Daniel Anthonys and Rochester followers of Garrison, William C. Bloss, Samuel D. Porter and Gideon Pitts of Honeoye, as well as John Brown. Because of his presence, the Underground Railroad flourished at his newspaper office at 25 Buffalo Street (now Main Street near the Genesee River), the family home at 4 Alexander (now a parking lot at 297) and their later home at 1023 South Avenue (now the site of No. 12 School, 999 South Avenue).

Even though their new home was a handsome nine-room brick house, it had been a tremendous hardship for Anna to leave Massachusetts, where she had a close-knit circle of friends. Shortly after the move, she traveled with her husband to an antislavery convention, and they were guests at the gracious home of Unitarian minister Reverend Samuel May in Syracuse. In the comfort and privacy of his home, Anna was relaxed and enjoyed seeing

The Douglass family's first home in Rochester, on Alexander Street. *Rochester Images, Rochester Public Library Local History Division.*

her friends from Boston. But in the 1840s, racism was strong in Rochester, and she usually stayed at home so Frederick could travel while she managed the household with the aid of a laundress.

Frederick Douglass worked out of the Talman Building, on Buffalo Street, which Mary Talman inherited after the death of her husband, John Talman. Mary E. Fitzhugh Talman was a daughter of William Fitzhugh, one of Rochester's founders, and Ann Smith's sister. (Ann Carroll Fitzhugh and Gerrit Smith, who were married in 1822, had eight children together.)

Horace McGuire, one of Douglass's newspaper employees, said it was not unusual to find fugitives sitting on the office stairs in the early morning. As soon as Douglass arrived, they were escorted to a safe place. Word of their need was sent out, and by nightfall, the escaped slaves were usually sent on to Oswego or Lewiston.

Mailings went out to Canada, Mexico, Australia and Great Britain. Unfortunately, the printing press they used for the *North Star* was inadequate, and subscriptions didn't cover production costs. Shortly after he and Anna bought their new house, Frederick took to the lecture circuit again in order to make ends meet.

The Talman Building on Buffalo Street in Rochester (circa 1860), where Douglass edited the *North Star. Rochester Images, Rochester Public Library Local History Division.*

At the end of April, Frederick Douglass wrote to Julia Griffiths in England, "I fear I have miscalculated in regard to the amount of support which would be extended to my enterprise...Things have not turned out at all as I expected."

The newspaper had seven hundred subscribers to support production costs of fifty-five dollars a week. He needed twenty-five dollars a week more for six months in order to keep it afloat and trusted that if he kept it for a year, he could sustain it permanently. He asked Julia's pardon in his lateness in replying to her letter. His agreement with Martin Delaney had been that Frederick would stay in Rochester and edit the paper, and Martin would travel and solicit subscriptions. Due to complications, Delaney had been unable fulfill his part, so Frederick was editing, lecturing and collecting subscriptions. He toured western New York starting on March 23 from Canandaigua, returning home on April 27.

At the end of June, Frederick Douglass wrote a letter to the "Dear Readers" of the *North Star* to explain his absence due to a tonsillectomy.

WOMEN'S RIGHTS CONVENTION

In mid-July, Frederick Douglass thanked abolitionist Quaker Elizabeth McClintock for her invitation to the proposed women's convention in Seneca Falls. He said he would attend and that he had happily also received a notice from Lucretia Mott.

On July 20, 1848, women's rights advocate Elizabeth Cady Stanton presented her Declaration of Sentiments to the first Women's Rights Convention in Seneca Falls, held in the Wesleyan Methodist Church. This church was founded in 1843 when church leaders of the Methodist ministry chose to ignore the issue of slavery in the interests of national unity. Pro-abolitionist members broke away and were joined by like-minded Presbyterians and Baptists. Wesleyan Methodist Church had immediately opened its doors to any abolitionist or reform group needing a place to meet.

When there was doubt whether the resolution for women's right to vote would pass, Stanton asked Frederick Douglass to address the convention. He compared his struggle against slavery to problems women faced. After he spoke, the resolution passed by a small majority. Out of one hundred signers, about twenty-three Quakers signed the Declaration of Sentiments, affirming the equality of men and women.

Amy Post wrote to Frederick Douglass and Martin Delaney in August 1848 to let them know that she held meetings every week in the Anti-Slavery rooms to "sew, knit, read and talk" while preparing for the big bazaar on December 20. "Indeed, I can scarcely wait from one Thursday to another...so strongly have the ties of friendship become cemented. Oh, the blessedness of Anti-slavery!— it not only makes friends at home, but the veriest friends of strangers."

After attending a conference in late August in Buffalo, Douglass traveled on a lecture tour in New England, New York State, Pennsylvania and Ohio to solicit subscriptions for the paper and to use his fees for its support.

In September 1848, on the tenth anniversary of his escape, Frederick Douglass published an open letter to Thomas Auld, listing all his grievances with his old master:

> *You well know that I wear stripes on my back inflicted by your direction; and that you, while we were brothers in the same church, caused this right hand, with which I am now penning this letter, to be closely tied to my left, and my person dragged at the pistol's mouth, fifteen miles, from the Bay side to Easton, to be sold like a beast in the market, for the alleged crime of*

intending to escape from your possession. At this moment, you are probably the guilty holder of at least three of my own dear sisters, and my only brother in bondage. These you regard as your property.

In it he also mentioned that his free children were going regularly to school:

Dear fellows! They are all in comfortable beds, and are sound asleep, perfectly secure under my own roof. There are no slaveholders here to rend my heart by snatching them from my arms, or blast a proud mother's dearest hopes by tearing them from her bosom. These dear children are ours—not to work up into rice, sugar and tobacco, but to watch over, regard and protect...

Anna mailed her husband fresh clothes while he traveled, so he was always well dressed. She was famous for her cooking, including "exalted" flaky beaten biscuits called Maryland biscuits, and preferred to wear a dark cotton dress and a red bandanna. Each time an issue of the paper was printed, Anna cooked a special meal. Rosetta later wrote, "Publication day was always a day for extra rejoicing as each weekly paper was seen as an arrow piercing the veil of gloom that shrouded her race. She felt it her duty to have the table well supplied with extra provisions that day, a custom we children fully appreciated."

As for local schools, Rochester's Board of Education had created separate public schools for black students. When the Douglass family moved to Rochester, the city school district had two separate schools for black children on Spring Street and North Washington Street, and Douglass chose not to send Rosetta so far from home.

The Board of Education wouldn't let the Douglass children enter City School No. 15, which at the time was on Alexander Street (now 217 Alexander Street), two short blocks from their house.

Years later, in his third autobiography, *Life and Times*, Douglass wrote:

My troubles attending the education of my children were not to end here. They were not allowed in the public school in the district in which I lived, owned property, and paid taxes, but were compelled, if they went to a public school, to go over to the other side of the city to an inferior colored school. I hardly need to say that I was not prepared to submit tamely to this proscription, any more than I had been to submit to slavery, so I had them taught at home for a while.

This building at 217 Alexander Street formerly housed City School No. 15. *Robert P. Meadows.*

Douglass hired a Quaker tutor, Miss Phoebe Thayer, to teach the younger children at home. In September 1848, Douglass enrolled Rosetta at the Seward Seminary, a private girls' school on Tracey Street (a side street a short block from their house, even closer than No. 15 School). When she first went to school, Douglass was away at the National Convention of Colored Citizens in Cleveland. He didn't know Rosetta wasn't allowed in the classroom with the white girls because of opposition from one parent: anti-abolitionist Horatio G. Warner.

The third week of September, Frederick Douglass wrote a letter about his displeasure at Rosetta's treatment to lawyer Horatio G. Warner, editor of the *Rochester Courier*. Miss Tracy had said she hoped that if Rosetta were instructed separately for a term, the pupils would have a chance to overcome their prejudice. Yet further inquiry showed that, despite biased questioning, none of the students objected to Rosetta's presence in the classroom; Miss Tracey had insisted there be no objections from the parents, and there was one.

Seward Seminary in Rochester, which Rosetta attended for a short time. *Rochester Images, Rochester Public Library Local History Division.*

Douglass wrote:

> *You are in a minority of* one. *You may not remain so; there are perhaps others, whom you may corrupt, and make as much like yourself in the blindness of prejudice, as any ordinarily wicked person can be. But you are still in a minority, and if I mistake not, you will be in a* despised minority—*You have already done serious injury to Seward Seminary. Three young ladies left the school immediately after the exclusion of my daughter, and I have heard of three more, who had intended to go, but who have now declined…I am also glad to inform you…that she "had not been excluded from Seward Seminary five hours, before she was gladly welcomed into another quite as respectable, and* equally *Christian to the one from which she was excluded."*

After Douglass sent Rosetta to Albany to continue her education, he began a campaign to end segregation in the Rochester city schools.

In early December, Frederick Douglass wrote to a supporter that he had been on a speaking tour for five weeks and would gladly visit Ohio in July 1849. He had traveled from late October through mid-November to Springfield, Lynn, New Bedford, Abington, Plymouth and Lowell, Massachusetts; then

The home of anti-abolitionist Horatio G. Warner was in a remote area, across from Mount Hope Cemetery in Rochester, New York. *Rochester Images, Rochester Public Library Local History Division.*

on to Providence, to the annual meeting of the Rhode Island Anti-Slavery Society; and back to Springfield and five more cities before returning to Rochester at the beginning of the month.

While he had been away on tour, Frederick Douglass had received "two elegantly framed portraits—one of my esteemed friend, Henry Highland Garnet, and the other of myself," and begged the senders to accept his heartfelt thanks. Theses supporters urged all opponents of slavery to hang portraits of Douglass and others in their parlors to show their solidarity. He printed their letter, with his reply in the *North Star* in mid-December. Garnet was an escaped slave who had been ordained as a Presbyterian minister and was pastor of the Liberty Street Presbyterian Church in Troy, New York.

From across the Atlantic Ocean, sisters Julia and Eliza Griffiths and others contributed eighty-two pounds from British women for the Rochester Anti-Slavery Bazaar, including boxes of donated items. Local supporters from Port Byron, Cayuga County, Darien, Genesee County and Henrietta in Monroe County also sent donations of all kinds.

Chapter 3
Alexander Street

I n the January 5, 1849 edition of the *North Star*, Frederick Douglass printed a letter from a critic from a "Farm nigh Athens, Ga." following up on the (September 1848) open letter to Thomas Auld:

> *It is always comprehended among us that the negroes are a peppery, irritable and proud and obdurate people, who, when they have a chance, would be sure to prove always irksome and often intolerable to European society…It seems to be fated to you, or to be impossible for you to act with that becoming propriety which should evince a worthy, and intelligent and pious people. Hence, many at the North wish you in Liberia, and many more slave-holders in the South wish the slaves colonized away in their patrimonial domains. All else is the result more of your character and conduct, than of color only.*

The editor's response had been: "The arguments—or rather the statements advanced…are simply ridiculous. It would be an insult to the common sense of the reader to answer them."

Frederick Douglass put a notice in the February 16, 1849 issue of the *North Star* that he and John S. Jacobs, a fugitive slave, were to hold antislavery meetings between February 12 and 23 in Henrietta, Mendon, Rush, Avon, Lima, West Bloomfield, Canandaigua, Rushville, Penn Yan, Prattsburg and Bath, New York. He requested that readers in these towns near Rochester find suitable locations where they could meet. Afterward, as an editorial in

HISTORICAL MARKER

HALLOCK HOUSE

Frederick Douglass often visited Quaker William Hallock at his home. The historic marker in front of this house reads:

Frederick Douglass often visited Quaker Wm. Hallock who induced him to reject John Brown's violent plans to free the slaves.

The Hallock House in Rush, New York. Owner William Hallock was a Quaker friend and supporter of Frederick Douglass. *Author's collection.*

the issue of March 9, 1849, he wrote his account of the lecture tour in cold and snowy weather.

Over one hundred years later, Bessie Hallock, a descendant of Quaker William Hallock, wrote of this tour, saying that Frederick Douglass had stopped at the Hallock House, now on Route 15A in Rush, Monroe County, while riding on horseback to give a talk in Lima. He and his host, William Hallock, a Quaker, who was known to give Douglass rides from his farm to places where he was to speak, carried on a conversation until noon, when

Douglass was invited to eat. Their lively conversation went on all afternoon, with the men differing not on the end to be gained but on the ways of gaining it. Douglass was very bitter at the time and attacked his opponents "without gloves."

Great-Grandfather Hallock believed in the Quaker way: "Thee can't make a man reform by calling him a scamp. Tell him what thee thinks is right, but don't attack his ideas. He is a man like thyself. Present thy case without rancor. Present thy case without bitterness, which only arouses the ire of thy opponent. Go at it gently."

After Douglass read the lecture he had planned to present the following night, Hallock shook his head and said Frederick might as well stay the night, as his talk had set them both to thinking deeply. The following night, Great-Grandfather and the boys attended the lecture. Afterward, back at the house, Hallock commented that it wasn't the same lecture Frederick had first read to him.

Douglass answered, "No, Mr. Hallock, it wasn't. You convinced me. I'll not show my bitterness again."

Based on Bessie Hallock's writing, some historians consider the Hallock House to be the birthplace of the civil rights movement in the United States.

At the end of March, Frederick Douglass wrote to supporter Gerrit Smith of his mistake in using half of the $2,000 he had received from supporters in England to buy a printing press, type cases and stands instead of contracting with an experienced printer. Frederick now found himself $200 in debt. He

FORMER SLAVE HARRIET A. JACOBS, who lived with her brother in Rochester from March 1849 to September 1850, was listed in the city directory as "Agent, Anti-Slavery Reading Rooms, over 25 Buffalo." Her brother, whom she called William, was a lecturer and organizer for the Massachusetts and New England Anti-Slavery Societies and had hoped to open a reading room and sell books there. For a few months, he was manager of the Anti-Slavery Office and Reading Room, but it did not succeed. Harriet lived for a year with Isaac and Amy Post. Later, in *Incidents in the Life of a Slave Girl*, published pseudonymously in 1861, she wrote of her life, born in 1813 as a slave in North Carolina. Along with Douglass's telling of his life, her autobiography of a black woman before the Civil War is one of the two strongest examples in the genre of slave narrative.

announced a week of speaking engagements in April between Rochester and Syracuse to repay the debt and his plan to leave the paper to his partner, William C. Nell. Douglass mentioned that the "dear little boy of ours" for whom he had cut short his lecture tour in late February in central New York "seems much better this morning. We have also a dear little girl under our roof—only one week old. Mrs. Douglass is doing very well—up nearly all day yesterday."

Anna Murray Douglass had given birth to their daughter Annie on March 22, 1849.

THE GRIFFITHS SISTERS

In April 1849, Frederick Douglass wrote to Amy and Isaac Post from the Post family homestead in Westbury, Long Island, "seated in the quiet—so pleasant after ten days of confusion in the city of New York. This is a beautiful place. The little lake lies sleeping lovingly at the right of the window—and all looks sweet quiet and quakerly around."

Douglass wrote that high winds from the west had prevented the steamer with the Griffiths sisters from arriving from England as scheduled five to seven days earlier. His success in increasing the circulation of the *North Star* had been encouraging, with a committee of ten having agreed to become subscription agents and forty to fifty signing up to receive it. (He also mentioned an antislavery meeting in Rochester that may have met in Harriet Jacob's antislavery reading room, which her brother John S. Jacobs was likely to attend.)

In May 1849, Julia Griffiths arrived from England with her younger sister Eliza and moved in with the family. Julia arrived with presents for all the children and plans to take charge of the paper. Frederick's close working relationship with her caused an interracial scandal in the antislavery movement.

Frederick Douglass traveled with both sisters, but the sight of a black man escorting white women on city streets was controversial. After Eliza got married and moved away, their unconventional friendship lost its protection from gossip.

When the family first moved to their Alexander Street home, they spent their time in the evenings playing chess or checkers and performing one-act plays. Rosetta played the piano while the others sang. At first Anna enjoyed this kind of family time at home and socializing with the Posts, but she withdrew from them after the Griffiths sisters arrived.

Julia Griffiths was known for wearing eccentric clothing and so much jewelry that people commented unfavorably. Douglass wrote later of those times:

> There were barriers erected against colored people in most other places of instruction and amusement in the city [of Rochester], and until I went there they were imposed without any apparent sense of injustice and wrong, and submitted to in silence; but one by one they have gradually been removed and colored people now enter freely, without hindrance or observation, all places of public resort. From the first I was cheered on and supported in my demands for equal rights by such respectable citizens as Isaac Post, Wm. Hallowell, Samuel D. Porter, Wm. C. Bloss, Benj. Fish, Asa Anthony, and many other good and true men of Rochester.

He also praised the groundwork done by the late Honorable Myron Holley, who had a marble monument in Rochester's Mount Hope Cemetery

> befitting his noble character. I know of no place in the Union where I could have located at the time with less resistance, or received a larger measure of sympathy and cooperation, and I now look back to my life and labors there with unalloyed satisfaction, and having spent a quarter century among its people, I shall always feel more at home there than anywhere else in this country.

In the late 1840s, the *North Star* had a circulation of about two thousand, with much of that support coming from friends in England. After the Griffiths sisters moved to the Douglass home, Julia became the business manager of the paper and suggested Douglass separate his personal finances from those of the paper.

Within a year, her tireless work brought the paper out of debt, and the circulation rose from two thousand to four thousand. Next to Griffiths and Douglass himself, the third most important figure in keeping the paper going was Gerrit Smith, whose generosity later increased after Douglass became a political abolitionist.

Frederick Douglass wrote to Amy Post from Niagara, New York, canceling his rigorous tour in Detroit on July 4, 5 and 6; Battle Creek on July 8 and 9; Chicago on July 12 through 15; onto Ohio to Sandusky on July 19, 20 and 21; Green Plain on July 22; Columbus on July 25; and ending in Cincinnati on July 28 to August 1. He had become sick with a fever and body aches in Detroit, and due to the intense heat there, he rested in Windsor, Canada, for three days before returning to Rochester. He did not think he could tour due to the cholera epidemic, caused by unsanitary open sewers and garbage-filled streets, which ravaged Midwestern cities in the summer of 1849 and caused 130 burials a day and 625 deaths in one week.

He had started the tour to Detroit accompanied by Charles Remond and Julia and Eliza Griffiths, writing that Julia was still ill "and Eliza is the only sound one of the company." He also wrote that "the Girls have just sent thirty dollars more towards holding up the *North Star*. I am now at no expense—they sustain me while I am ill—and until I get strong."

The Douglass family had bought the house on Alexander Street for $1,000 in April 1848, but despite Anna's best efforts, Frederick had trouble separating the business expenses from the mortgage. Eliza Griffiths then bought the mortgage in August 1849. Later, after her marriage in April 1851, she signed the mortgage over to her sister Julia, who declared the debt paid off in March 1853. By their actions, the Griffiths sisters protected the Douglass home from creditors for four years.

GOOD NEWS INDEED

In early September 1849, Frederick Douglass wrote another open letter to Thomas Auld, including his own home address. Frederick wrote:

> *I have been told by a person intimately acquainted with your affairs, and upon whose word I can rely, that you have ceased to be a slave-holder, and have emancipated all your slaves, except my poor old grandmother, who is now too old to sustain herself in freedom; and that you have taken her from the desolate hut in which she formerly lived, into your own kitchen, and are now providing for her in a manner becoming a man and a Christian. This, sir, is indeed good news…I shall conclude this letter again expressing my sincere gratitude at the magnanimous deed with which your name is now associated*[.]

The source of Douglass's information is unknown, but according to the 1850 census, Thomas Auld still kept four women and two men between the ages of eight and twenty-four as slaves. Meanwhile, his aged grandmother, Betsey Bailey, reportedly died in November 1849.

Frederick Douglass expressed thanks for a generous donation from a supporter in November 1849. He also mentioned that he and his wife had five children, of which two boys, Lewis and Frederick, and one daughter went to school.

It is likely that Rosetta, who could sew every stitch in her father's shirts by the time she was ten, learned to sew from her aunt Charlotte Murray. Rosetta also worked for a time in her father's office when she was eleven, folding papers and writing wrappers. As she got older and more skilled, she became his personal secretary, writing down the editorials and lectures he dictated.

A SUPPORTER IN BELFAST wrote to Frederick Douglass in late December 1849, apologizing for her inability to collect enough items in time for the annual Rochester Fair. There was significant competition from fairs in Ireland due to the poverty crisis there. Lest he think Belfast's support had faded, she enclosed a copy of the "monster petition," which was signed by 6,118 women in Ireland and sent to Queen Victoria on behalf of the victims of the African slave trade.

The Rochester Anti-Slavery Fair, which had been planned for that December, was rescheduled to late January 1850 to avoid conflicting with similar fairs and allow more time for collecting donations. The items for sale from Europe were often expensive and popular due to Julia Giffiths' presence.

1850

In early February 1850, Amy Post expressed her dismay at Frederick Douglass's write-up in the most recent issue of the *North Star* stating that the Rochester Fair was a financial failure as well as a moral disappointment. Revenue had been $220, which after expenses came to $117. Right beneath this accounting, he reported the proceeds of the Boston Anti-Slavery Fair, which had taken in $3,300.

Amy wrote:

> *Yet we would not dispise* [sic] *even the sum of one hundred dollars, but rejoice to have it to add to other hundred's that have been raised and used in the cause, during the past year, and in point of morals, I believe we have no reason to conclude, that because some rudeness appeared among a group of boys one evening, the whole tendency was immoral, was it nothing*

JULIA GRIFFITHS' SISTER Eliza and other boarders, including John Dick, also stayed with the Douglass family. When Eliza and John married and moved to Canada in 1850, Julia's living there alone caused a scandal, and the growing hostility led her to board with John and Mary Porter.

IN AUGUST 1850, a month before the Fugitive Slave Bill became law, Frederick Douglass spoke at a convention in Cazenovia, New York. The Fugitive Slave Convention was attended by two thousand people, including thirty fugitives, who pledged to raise money for the defense of William Chaplin, who had been arrested in Rockville, Maryland, for helping two slaves escape. A few weeks later, in Syracuse, Douglass and others raised $350 for Chaplin's defense.

that one hundred people, of all classes and colours sat down to one table, and the most perfect decorum and order prevailed.

She signed it, "Thy soarely agrieved [*sic*] friend."

He replied that his intent was to share the facts, but he did not despise the money raised.

Gerrit Smith wrote to Frederick Douglass of his outrage at reading in the May 30 issue of the *North Star*, which included the account of the assault and death threats Douglass had received in New York City. Frederick had traveled there with Eliza and Julia Griffiths to attend the annual meeting of the American Anti-Slavery Society at the Broadway Tabernacle on May 7. He had stayed another week to attend a fundraising fair for the paper, and while walking along Battery Park with the Griffiths sisters, he had been verbally harassed by white men for walking as an equal with white women. He was savagely beaten until one of the women succeeded in calling over a policeman.

Smith was sympathetic and wrote: "Despair not, however, my dear brother—All will be made right, and in due time. The religion of Jesus—the religion of the Bible—that will prevail; and when it does prevail, it will make all right. For it is not a slavery or caste religion; but a religion of love, and freedom, and equality."

The passing of the Fugitive Slave Act of 1850 quadrupled the traffic on the Underground Railroad as abolitionist speakers in the South advocated insurrection and abolition.

The Compromise of 1850 admitted California as a free state and prohibited the sale of slaves in the District of Columbia, where it had thrived. The compromise included a new Fugitive Slave Law, called the "bloodhound bill," that expanded the power of the federal government to protect the interests of slave owners and mandated the return of fugitive slaves. After the Fugitive Slave Law was passed, slave catchers swarmed north to kidnap and sell into slavery any freed black who could not produce his or her papers on demand. Hundreds of terrified free blacks fled New York City, Philadelphia and Boston to Canada in the first few months. After this slave law was passed, more whites joined the Underground Railroad, which had been a predominantly black network. Prominent attorneys and preachers gave money for more stations and routes. Churches and schools were used for antislavery meetings.

While the Slave Law of 1793 had given strong incentives to return fugitives to their owners, the Fugitive Slave Law of 1850 provided a $1,000 fine and another $1,000 for each fugitive assisted, as well as a five-year prison term. Rochester's black population dropped between 1850 and 1860 as free blacks fled to Canada, including 112 of 118 members of the Abyssinian Baptist Church.

During the 1830s, northern cities had well-led, well-staffed and well-funded safe stations, which became highly organized and aggressive as fugitive slaves and free blacks were kidnapped by slave catchers and sold into slavery. Philadelphia directed nine thousand runaways between 1830 and 1860. The number of jailed fugitives and rescue attempts surged after Congress passed the Fugitive

Rochester artist Maria Friske's mural shows slaves fleeing toward the North Star. *Always Know Your Neighbor* is on Pembroke Street in Rochester. *Robert P. Meadows.*

PRESIDENT MILLARD FILLMORE, who met and married his wife, Abigail, in New York State's Finger Lakes area, served from 1850 to 1853. Abigail Powers Fillmore lobbied for funds for the first library in the White House. She was one of his most trusted advisors, a strong believer in the abolition of slavery and was opposed to the Fugitive Slave Law of 1850.

Slave Law in 1850. Before that, railroad agents and abolitionists had been considered dangerous extremists.

After the Fugitive Slave Act of 1850 was passed, Amy Post's friend Lucy Colman wrote of going to Canada with her. Coleman believed "all but 1,000" of 40,000 refugees in Canada knew Amy by name.

For many black abolitionists, the new law broke their faith in nonviolence and the chance of a peaceful end to slavery. Douglass later wrote bitterly that the true remedy for the fugitive slave law was a good revolver, a steady hand and a determination to shoot down any man attempting to kidnap.

1851

In the 1850s, the week following Christmas—and in general, the weeks from mid-December to mid-January—was a time for celebration and civic giving. The Buffalo Ladies' Anti-Slavery Society held a benefit on New Year's Eve to support the *North Star*. Although the crowds were small, due to short notice and competition from events like the Fireman's Ball the same evening, they were grateful for Frederick Douglass's opening speeches on three consecutive evenings. The society forwarded fifty-four dollars on January 10, 1851, with words of continued support.

The *North Star* newspaper was issued weekly and soon had 3,000 subscribers that eventually peaked at 4,500. Publication cost eighty dollars a week, so to make ends meet, Frederick Douglass gave lectures in the Corinthian Hall, owned by William R. Reynolds.

In a letter to Gerrit Smith, Frederick Douglass thanked Smith for his donation of fifteen dollars and mentioned he was eager to hear Smith's opinion of two lectures Douglass had already given in Rochester.

Douglass had started to deliver a series of nine speeches in Rochester's Corinthian Hall on Sunday evenings, starting December 1 and 8, 1850, and

Frederick Douglass supported the *North Star* by lecturing at Corinthian Hall in downtown Rochester. *Rochester Images, Rochester Public Library Local History Division.*

published them as a pamphlet in January 1851. He was "seriously intending" to publish all nine lectures in book form and appreciated Smith's offer of twenty-five dollars toward that end: "The fact that negroes are turning Book makers may possibly serve to remove the impression that they are fit only as Boot blackers & although they may not *shine* in the former profession as they have long done in the latter, I am not without hope that they will do themselves good by making the effort."

Douglass mentioned the meeting on January 16 of the Western New York Anti-Slavery Society and a resolution about the pro-slavery stands built into the U.S. Constitution. He also sent kind regards to Mrs. Smith (Ann Carroll Fitzhugh Smith).

The Douglass family's savings account grew steadily after the publication of his first book. In the spring, Douglass wrote to Gerrit Smith that he would be able to pay off his house in a few months. During the 1850s, Douglass's lecture fee was twenty-five dollars.

On May 1, Frederick Douglass sent an enthusiastic letter to Gerrit Smith about Smith's proposal to merge the *North Star* with John Thomas's *Liberty Party* paper in which Smith had invested $3,500, to no avail, in the last year. While he was not immediately concerned about his own paper, Douglass did see the advantages of joining with Smith's and liked Smith's plan to have a good paper as well as a good-looking one.

Douglass preferred to publish it in Rochester because his house would be paid off in a few months, his family was unwilling to move again and he did not want to live away from them. He liked Smith's new motto yet thought it best to have the paper in his own name to avoid criticisms about Smith's wealth. The last issue of the *Liberty Party* was printed on June 5.

On May 15, Frederick Douglass wrote to Gerrit Smith about some problems with the merger of the two papers. He also suggested having a female correspondent: Sallie Holley, daughter of prominent abolitionist the late Myron Holley, an 1851 graduate of Oberlin College who became a traveling lecturer for the American Anti-Slavery Society.

On June 9, 1851, Gerrit Smith wrote, in reply, of his joy at learning that Frederick Douglass and John Thomas had united their papers into one and that Samuel Ward would be corresponding editor. "If you, who have been a slave, cannot speak effectively against slavery, who can?" Smith congratulated Douglass on the new motto for the *Frederick Douglass Paper*: "All Rights for All."

Frederick Douglass thanked Gerrit Smith on June 10 for the $200 received, as well as "the good letter you have sent me for my New paper." He published an editorial in the June 12 edition of the *North Star* that his paper was merging. Douglass then mailed a proof of the last copy of the *North Star* to Smith on June 18. The first issue of the *Frederick Douglass Paper* came out on June 26, 1851.

That July, Frederick Douglass had been so sick with a fever, stomach problems and sore throat that he feared throat problems would restrict his speaking abilities, making him eager to work on the paper. He thanked Gerrit Smith for a letter that Julia Griffiths had handed him containing $100. He apologized for "writing with a feeble and trembling hand this being my first letter since my convalescence."

Hostility against colored boys was so strong that the Douglass family kept them close to home. Over one summer vacation, when Frederick wondered what the boys could do with their time, Anna suggested they work in his office. At the ages of eleven and nine, Lewis and Fred Jr. were perched on blocks and given their first lesson in printer's ink, besides carrying papers and mailing them.

In response to Julia Griffiths' appeal, Frederick Douglass thanked Gerrit Smith for his generosity—"but necessity, my friend, would listen to no regrets.

I was under the hammer, and my friend Julia seeing it cried out in my behalf. You came to my help, and I am on my legs again. I bless you for it."

Douglass also mentioned he expected to receive much support from the Female Antislavery Society. "The Ladies who compose it are persons upon whom I can rely...Julia Griffiths is highly pleased with the results of her labors in forming this Society."

In September 1851, Frederick Douglass wrote a note to Samuel Porter (first president of the Western New York Anti-Slavery Society in 1835): "My Dear Sir, There are three men now at my house—who are in great peril. I am unwell. I need your advice. Please come at once." In order to disguise his name, he initialed it "D.F."

Douglass was again sick for most of the month of November with an inflamed throat. His November 27 editorial was entitled "The Colored People and Our Paper": "It is for you to say whether you can dispense with the services of the only Journal

HARRIET BEECHER STOWE, who had subscribed to Douglass's paper in 1847, wrote to him in July 1851 for his input as a former laborer in the cotton fields. This contact was the beginning of her long friendship with him. At the time, she was writing a series of articles entitled, "Uncle Tom's Cabin, or Life among the Lowly," for the *National Era*, which ran weekly from June 5, 1851, until April 1, 1852. This was the first known correspondence between two of the most famous antislavery writers of the day. Harriet Beecher Stowe started a trend by using slang and local dialects in her writing.

Harriet Tubman, the famous Underground Railroad conductor, met the Douglass family while helping slaves escape to Canada. *Rochester Images, Rochester Public Library Local History Division.*

THE FEMALE ANTI-SLAVERY SOCIETY, which had been formed in Rochester in 1835, was a social club that considered slavery a sin and called for its immediate abolition. The new group was a community sewing circle and antislavery group that sought to cooperate with everyone opposed to slavery. It had about twenty-five members.

Harriet Beecher Stowe gave advice to the Rochester Anti-Slavery Sewing Society on the publication of its fundraising book. Her letter (now in the Porter collection in the University of Rochester's Rare Books Collection) shows her suggestion for the name of their fundraiser: Autographs for Freedom. In 1851, Julia Griffiths, a founder of the Rochester Ladies' Anti-Slavery Sewing Circle and its secretary, edited its two publications, *Autographs for Freedom*, an anthology of abolitionist writings.

in this country which is, in every sense, identified with the interests and happiness of yourselves." To his disappointment, "not one colored man in the United States responded to the earnest appeal of the proposer." Douglass did receive a pledge of ten dollars from a supporter in early December.

Militant abolitionist John Brown sent a letter of encouragement to Douglass in mid-December, and John Brown Jr. also wrote asking that a bill for his two-dollar subscription be sent to Vernon, Ohio, where he would seek subscribers upon his return there.

One of Frederick Douglass's earliest supporters in Rochester, social activist and nurseryman Benjamin Fish, sent two dollars to support the paper for the coming year, "not because I agree with all it sends forth, for I see many things in it with which I disagree, and some which I disapprove, but I do not look for perfection in any paper, and with all its faults, I believe it to be doing *good anti-slavery* work, and for this I wish it to be sustained, and *well* sustained."

Harriet Tubman, who had escaped from slavery in 1848, made almost twenty trips over the next ten years into the South. From 1848 to 1858, she led slaves to Canada by hiding them in barns, cellars, attics and closets. During that time, she met Frederick and Anna's family because both Douglass homes had hiding places.

In December 1851, Tubman brought a group of eleven, including her brother and his wife, to Canada. It is likely they stayed on Alexander Street because Frederick wrote in his autobiography, "On one occasion I had eleven fugitives at the same time under my roof."

Chapter 4

Grand Avenue

1852

Later in life, Rosetta Douglass Sprague wrote that her father was home so seldom that her mother treated him like one of their many guests, including Julia Griffiths, who stayed with them from the spring of 1849 to January 1852. At different times, Anna also cared for four other boys who became members of the family circle. She took care of their clothing the same as her own children's, and "they delighted in calling her MOTHER."

In an uncomfortable start to the New Year, Frederick Douglass replied on January 12 to Samuel D. Porter:

> *When the city you allege to be full of scandalous reports implicating Miss G. and me, shall put—"those reports" into a definite shape—and present a responsible person to back them, it will be time enough for me to attempt to refute them…You and I have been friends during the last two or three years…It seems to me that a friendly word might have been, ere this, whispered to me—apprizeing me of these "scandalous reports"—and advising me how to allay them.*

He wrote to Porter that, of her own free will, Miss Griffiths had boarded with another family for almost two months: "I am in no way responsible for her words, her deeds or her dress…Still I do feel that she has a just claim upon my gratitude, respect and friendship."

Frederick Douglass wrote to Gerrit Smith in early February, "My health is improving and I am on my legs again. My joints have not yet attained their wonted elasticity…My hands are somewhat stiff and swollen—Yet you see I can use my pen, which to me is a source of much happiness. I look forward to warm weather for complete restoration—but until then, I shall play the *old* man." He also mentioned Mrs. Smith's climbing the long dark stairs to his office, and his worry that she had overextended herself, but that Julia was delighted to see her, and they "rode up from the office to our new home together."

Douglass was still recovering from the sore throat that had troubled him since November.

It must have cheered Douglass on the day in February when he received a note from a Quaker farmer and Underground Railroad agent from Williamson, New York: "I herewith enclose two dollars. Better late than never."

In writing to Gerrit Smith about the Rochester Ladies' Anti-Slavery Society's upcoming Grand Festival and Bazaar at the same time as the Grand Anti-Slavery Convention, Frederick Douglass said, "My dear Sir, you MUST *yes*, you must (if you possibly can), attend the convention in this city on the 18 & 19 March."

But on March 12, Frederick Douglass wrote to Smith, "I am taken by the announcement in it, like a ship at sea, by a head wind—*all aback*! Right bravely have we dashed through the waves of opposition until now;—but your giving up the idea of being at our Festival has deranged our whole ship's deck—and cast over us a cloud."

Despite Douglass's worries, Smith attended the festival, giving a talk the night before on temperance in Corinthian Hall. A few days afterward, Douglass wrote to him, "Your visit to Rochester has done good both to the cause of temperance and to Antislavery. The festival was highly successful, and has left a good impression."

In regards to the resolution—that the New York State Anti-Slavery Society ally itself with the American Anti-Slavery Society in Boston—which was defeated, Douglass wrote:

> *I am persuaded that there is a desire to provoke me into a controversy with them. They accuse me now, openly, of having sold myself to one Gerrit Smith Esq. and to have changed my views—more in consequence of your purse than your arguments! These things are disagreeable but they do not move me.*

Following up on a note from famous poet Henry Wadsworth Longfellow to Susan Porter, president of the Rochester Ladies' Anti-Slavery Society, Frederick Douglass wrote to Longfellow asking him to contribute twenty lines toward anything on slavery. Mrs. Porter had urged Douglass to write to Longfellow himself, but without success. Longfellow had already contributed to a similar fundraising gift book, *The Liberty Bell*, which was edited by Maria W. Chapman of Boston.

After having been invited to dinner by Gerrit Smith's sister-in-law and husband, Douglass wrote to Smith:

THE ROCHESTER LADIES' Anti-Slavery Society netted $407 in proceeds from its sale at that Anti-Slavery Festival, donating $233 to Douglass. He sent his "profound gratitude" to Susan F. Porter, president of the society, for its donation and "important services to the Antislavery cause in Rochester."

The New York State Anti-Slavery Society was formed on March 19, 1852, in Rochester. It condemned slavery as a crime, religious leaders who supported it and those who voted for slaveholders or those who failed to support abolition.

Now, what is the world coming to! Besides, I was not treated with a mere formal courtesy—but with evident kindness, such as I should receive under your own comprehensive roof. [Their] Dear Little Daughter...a lovely child, came to me, smiled, and played willingly with my sable hand;—Seeing apparently nothing in my color, form or features, to repel her.

In regard to meeting a former acquaintance, Douglass wrote of his early years as a speaker: "I, however, at that time, lived in the whirl and excitement of a lecturing life, and soon forgot" having met him. He also mentioned getting ready for the antislavery convention from April 27 to 29 in Cincinnati.

NEW FARM

In the summer of 1852, Gerrit Smith's wife, Ann, was criticized for climbing up the dark stairs to Frederick Douglass's office to surprise Julia Griffiths with a ride out to the Douglass family's new farm "high on a hill outside of town."

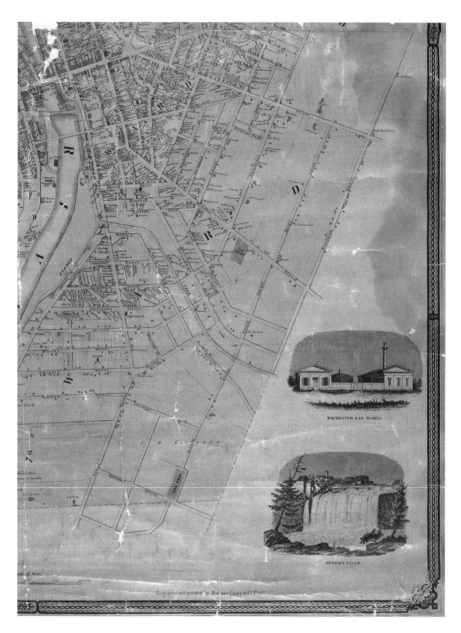

Southeast quadrant of Rochester in 1852. The Douglass homestead was in a remote location at the edge of the city limits. *Rochester Images, Rochester Public Library Local History Division.*

The view of downtown Rochester in the 1850s that the Douglass family would have seen. *Rochester Images, Rochester Public Library Local History Division.*

Frederick Douglass told the Rochester Ladies' Anti-Slavery Society at its Independence Day celebration in Corinthian Hall, "This Fourth of July is yours, not mine. You may rejoice; I must mourn."

That year, the talk was held on a Monday because the Fourth of July fell on a Sunday, which was considered the Lord's Day. The speech, attended by five to six hundred people, was so successful that the gathering unanimously voted to thank him formally for it. He printed the full text in the *Frederick Douglass Paper* (*FDP*), filling nine columns, and also published seven hundred copies as a pamphlet that became one of his best-remembered statements.

Two days later, Douglass wrote to Gerrit Smith, "My friend Julia tells me it was *excellent!*" A week later, he thanked Smith for his letter to Miss Griffiths containing twenty-five dollars toward the publication of the pamphlet. Despite his worry that Julia Griffiths "sometimes seems too urgent on my behalf. I must tell you however that I really am desireous to make some money as well as do some good with that speech."

In a letter to Amy Post in early August, Frederick Douglass mentioned cholera. Rochester was hit with another epidemic that killed 450 people. City officials had been unprepared and ordered an investigation that traced it to the open sewers and piles of garbage in crowded slums. He told Post, "My advice is be calm. Do not allow yourself to be alarmed…We are all subjects—parts of a great *whole*—in the hands of a Supreme power—and

FIVE TO SIX HUNDRED people had paid twelve and a half cents to hear the speech, which was so popular that seven hundred copies of a pending pamphlet were subscribed that same day. It was considered the greatest antislavery oration ever given.

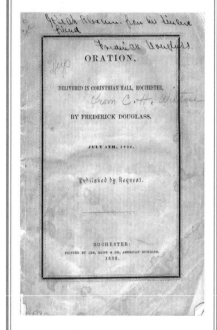

One of the original seven hundred pamphlets printed after Douglass's stirring speech in July 1852. *Rochester Museum & Science Center collection.*

you and I have decided that power is *good*. Leave all to the Supreme *good* and be calm."

Hardly a women's rights meeting occurred in the 1850s without Frederick Douglass as one of the principal speakers. Partly due to him, the first National Woman's Rights Convention of 1850 had adopted the slogan "Equality before the law without distinction of sex or color." In many ways, he brought the rights of blacks and women together. When Gerrit Smith once asked Susan B. Anthony how he might best keep himself informed about the women's movement, she told him to read Douglass's paper.

Frederick Douglass and women's rights advocate Susan B. Anthony, who had become close friends, argued publicly over who needed the vote most: women or black men. She was unwavering in her belief that equality for black men and the drive for women's suffrage be reached as one goal. When Elizabeth Cady Stanton said, "I would not talk of negroes or women, but of citizens," Douglass agreed with her fully.

A turning point in Susan B. Anthony's life had been being chosen by the Rochester Daughters of Temperance as delegate to a state convention of the Sons of Temperance in Albany in 1852. She was allowed to have a seat on the convention floor but not to speak. She and other delegates left the convention and organized the Woman's State Temperance Society. Her father, who owned cotton mills and factories, was a temperance advocate and supporter of

Susan B. Anthony became Douglass's lifelong friend starting in Rochester.

Susan B. Anthony's parents, Daniel and Lucy Anthony. *Rochester Images, Rochester Public Library Local History Division.*

DURING THE 1850s, the work of the Underground Railroad became known as the "League of Freedom," "Liberty League" or "American Mysteries," which had fourteen "True Bands" in Canada.

abolition, and Susan had grown up believing in racial and gender equality. She had also experienced sex discrimination as a schoolteacher whose pay was much less than male teachers. In 1845, her family had moved to a farm west of Rochester that had become a favorite gathering place for Quakers and Rochester reformers, including Douglass, with whom she became life-long friends.

Elizabeth Cady Stanton, Matilda Joslyn Gage and Lucretia Mott were among the leaders of the women's rights cause. Stanton and Mott organized the convention in Seneca Falls in 1848. Gage and Susan B. Anthony joined them in 1852.

Frederick Douglass spent the month of October 1852 working for Gerrit Smith's election to Congress as an independent. On October 1, he, along with William Lloyd Garrison, Lucretia Mott, Gerrit Smith and Lucy Stone, addressed about five thousand people at the first-anniversary celebration in Syracuse of the October 9, 1851 rescue of William "Jerry" McHenry.

In early October, Douglass attended eighteen meetings in twelve towns in Tompkins County, southeast of Rochester, and then campaigned near Gerrit Smith's home in Peterboro, New York. He addressed his readers in the October 25 issue, apologizing for his absence while on the campaign trail. In early November, he wrote to Gerrit Smith of his great joy at Smith's winning the election.

The National Council of Colored Men, held in Rochester in 1853, was one of the most representative and intelligent national conventions up to that time. This convention clearly defined opposition to the relief of colored freedmen through emigration. It proposed plans for an industrial college; a registry of colored mechanics, artisans and businessmen throughout the Union; and a publication committee to collect facts, statistics, laws, historical records and biographies of colored people and all books by colored people.

The Rochester Ladies' Anti-Slavery Society was one of the most active in the movement. For Julia Griffiths' collection of antislavery statements by celebrities with facsimile autographs, Frederick contributed a sixty-five-page novella, *The Heroic Slave*, that was his only work of fiction. Griffiths edited two volumes of *Autographs for Freedom* that came out in 1853 and 1854.

HIS SECOND BOOK

In 1855, in his second autobiography, *My Bondage and My Freedom*, Frederick aimed to clarify some of the harsh depictions of the first one. He mentioned Thomas Auld's promise to free him at age twenty-five, which at the time he had believed was too good to be true. He also softened his descriptions of Thomas and Hugh Auld, knowing that Thomas could have sold him to Florida for his attempted escape and didn't and that Hugh had given him room and board for several years.

Although he did receive the least amount of food and harshest treatment most regularly from another slave, Aunt Katy, and the worst treatment for a short time under Covey, in this second book, Frederick admitted that much of his childhood had been happy. Most of the corrections in his life story were overlooked, while sensational events were repeated at the expense of this more balanced account.

Harriet Beecher Stowe sent a twenty-five-dollar donation to the Rochester Anti-Slavery Sewing Society that year.

In 1856, Frederick Douglass's early mentor, the Reverend Thomas James, returned to Rochester. James took charge of AME Zion Church, which needed many repairs, and raised a fund of $600 for it. James had been pastor of AME Zion from 1829 to 1835. He had been ordained and founded AME Zion on Favor Street in 1833 and was again its pastor from 1856 to 1862.

Thomas James (1804–1891) had come from Canada to Rochester in 1823 and became a member of the African Methodist Episcopal Society that opened that year in Rochester. He worked in a warehouse of the Hudson &

Portrait of seasoned orator Frederick Douglass, circa 1856. *Rochester Images, Rochester Public Library Local History Division.*

St. Boniface Church, on the southeast side of the city, was at the heart of the neighborhood of German immigrants. *Rochester Images, Rochester Public Library Local History Division.*

Erie Line, using the winter months when the Erie Canal was closed to study. James was active in the antislavery movement from its beginnings in western New York and New England; had attended the first anti-slavery convention in Rochester; and founded a church in New Bedford, Massachusetts.

In 1857, Frederick Douglass, Samuel Porter and others succeeded in getting the city to integrate all its schools by race and sex a year before statewide integration took effect. Up until that time, city boys and girls were taught in separate classrooms. That year, the Rochester Public Schools ruled that Annie Douglass could attend her all-white neighborhood public school.

From 1857 to 1859, Annie attended School 13, which her father's secretary called the German public school because of the many German immigrants in southeast Rochester. Annie wrote, the "German children like me very much but I have gone a head [*sic*] of them and they been there much longer than me too."

JOHN BROWN

Militant abolitionist John Brown stayed with the Douglass family on South Avenue for three weeks in February 1858. They had first met at Brown's home in Springfield, Massachusetts, in November 1847, when Douglass had spent a night and a day under his roof. Douglass wrote, "I never felt myself in the presence of a stronger religious influence than while in this man's house." From that time on, Brown considered Douglass his chief Negro confidante. Brown's eastern campaign was started in Frederick and Anna's house on the hill.

While John Brown stayed at the Douglass home in Rochester, Annie, age nine, who was described as "a bright and impish child," became very fond of him. Charlie Douglass, fourteen, who also helped his father by delivering the paper, was briefly a messenger for John Brown.

Brown insisted on paying board, so Douglass charged him three dollars a week. It was there that Brown first met Shields Greene, an uneducated, escaped slave from South Carolina whom people called "Emperor" because of his royal bearing. Greene lived with the Douglass family and worked as a clothes cleaner and presser in a laundry on Spring Street.

Like many leading Negroes of his day, Douglass believed in John Brown but not in his plan to end slavery by creating a refuge for freed slaves in the mountains of Virginia.

When Annie Douglass was nine, she became fond of John Brown during his stay with the family. *Rochester Images, Rochester Public Library Local History Division.*

A short time later, in April 1858, John Brown first met Harriet Tubman in St. Catharine's, Ontario, Canada, where she was living. Tubman willingly shared her escape routes from the South with Brown, who organized a meeting of a secret convention in Chatham, Ontario, where about two thousand fugitives lived. Tubman suggested he set July 4, 1858, as the date for his attack on the South.

John Brown met Frederick Douglass and Shields Greene again in the summer of 1859 near a farm Brown was renting in Maryland, across from Harpers Ferry. Again, Douglass opposed Brown's plan to attack the armory at Harpers Ferry and left, but Greene stayed.

Because of letters between Frederick Douglass and John Brown, some considered Douglass guilty by association and wanted him arrested and tried for treason after Brown's attack on Harpers Ferry in October 1859. Douglass was speaking in Philadelphia and would have been seized almost immediately if a friendly telegraph operator in Philadelphia hadn't delayed the delivery of a telegram for the city sheriff to arrest him.

The telegraph operator's tactic gave Douglass the chance to rush from where he was staying and take a steamer to New York City and then a ferry to Hoboken. The next day, supporter Ottilie Assing sent a telegram addressed to a telegraph operator in Rochester whom Douglass trusted telling Anna and Frederick's son Lewis to secure important papers at the house that linked Douglass to Brown. Assing borrowed a carriage and drove him to Paterson, New Jersey, to board a train up the west side of the Hudson

This painting, *Port of Genesee*, from the 1850s, shows the way the port looked at the time of Douglass's escape. *Rochester Images, Rochester Public Library Local History Division.*

and on to Rochester. Once in Rochester, Amy and Isaac Post took him after dark to the wharf below the lower falls and put him on boat for Canada.

After John Brown's expedition was routed by Colonel Robert E. Lee, a United States marshal traveled to Rochester to arrest Frederick Douglass as a conspirator in the plot. On the Rochester-bound train, the officer met Judge Henry Selden, who had practiced law in Rochester for many years. The marshal confided his mission to Selden, who happened to be one of Douglass's few neighbors.

Judge Selden, who became a lieutenant governor under President Abraham Lincoln, left the train with the marshal and took him to the taproom of the Eagle Hotel. Several hours later, Selden left the drunken marshal, got word to Douglass that a warrant had been issued for his arrest and then loaned Douglass a horse so he could flee. Because of this tip, Douglass left quickly for Canada and then England.

The Eagle Hotel in downtown Rochester is where Judge Seldon delayed the marshal who was sent to arrest Frederick Douglass. *Rochester Images, Rochester Public Library Local History Division.*

Douglass spent several weeks lecturing in Canada before he sailed to England. He then endured a rough voyage for two weeks on the *Scotia* and arrived in Great Britain, where he was "beyond the reach of…Virginia's prisons." Since the English public was well aware of the events at Harpers Ferry and his plight, he traveled around the country as a speaker.

At the time of John Brown's trial, Susan B. Anthony sold tickets to a meeting at the Corinthian Hall to protest his possible hanging. Instead, three hundred people attended the meeting to mourn Brown's death. Despite strong Quaker teachings against the use of violence, because two of her brothers had served with Brown in Kansas to keep it a free state, Anthony considered him a hero and a martyr in the fight to end slavery. Southern whites thought John Brown was a violent fanatic; northern abolitionists hailed him as a martyr.

After Brown's death in early December 1859, Frederick Douglass said, "They could kill him, but they could not answer him." Years later, in a speech at Harpers Ferry, Douglass said:

> *If John Brown did not end the war that ended slavery, he did, at least, begin the war that ended slavery. If we look over the dates, places, and men for which this honor is claimed, we shall find not Carolina, but Virginia, not Fort Sumter, but Harpers Ferry and the arsenal, not Major [Robert] Anderson, but John Brown began the war that ended American slavery, and made this a free republic.*

Douglass called Brown's actions the logical result of slaveholding persecutions. He understood better than any of his white abolitionist colleagues that slavery was an institution built on violence and maintained by the fear of violence.

When John Brown was born in 1800, there were about one million men, women and children in slavery in the United States. At the time of his death by hanging on December 2, 1859, slavery had spread from the Atlantic Ocean to the Rio Grande, and from the Ohio River to the Gulf of Mexico, with over four million enslaved men, women and children.

Ottilie Assing

After reading Douglass's second autobiography, Ottilie Assing (1819–1884), a half-Jewish German journalist, visited him at his home in 1856. Because of the relief from gossip after Julia Griffiths' departure a year earlier, he did not invite her to move to Rochester. Over the winter of 1856 to 1857, she rented two rooms in Hoboken, New Jersey, in a spacious and comfortable house owned by Mrs. Marks, an older German woman. Assing lived there until 1865, with Douglass as a frequent guest. He and Mrs. Marks had a keen liking for each other.

Douglass invited Assing to the family home for the summer in 1857 so she could translate *My Bondage and My Freedom* into German. Frederick then wrote to her sister Ludmilla for help in finding a publisher, and the second autobiography was published in Hamburg in 1860. Frederick and Ottilie had an intense partnership as two people who valued the importance of learning and advancement. Scholar William McFeely wrote that it was impossible to determine whether they had more than a close working relationship.

Based on letters not yet available to McFeely, author Maria Diedrich claims otherwise. Assing was brought up to believe that women had the same right to professional training as men. Her parents prepared their daughters for active professional lives, including writing well and speaking several foreign languages, so they could make a living anywhere in the world.

One of their aunts, Rahel Varnhagen, was a pioneer for women's liberation in Germany. Their physical and intellectual mobility didn't fit contemporary views of womanhood. Diedrich attributes the veil of secrecy around Douglass and Assing's relationship to segregation, which allowed them to be together out of the public gaze of white society.

Ottilie Assing was more than a translator. She was full of stories that she shared in magical performances with the Douglass children. Not only did she and Frederick read out loud to each other, but she also started to teach him German and played the piano to his violin. She reached out to him, to the entire family, and continued to correspond with Rosetta for many years.

Family life wasn't smooth in those years when Frederick was often away, and Anna shouldered the care of the house and children—in poor health. Anna had barely felt the relief of Griffiths' absence when Assing arrived. Whether it is true or not that Anna was more comfortable in the kitchen than in the dining room, it may also have been her way of coping with middle-class white guests who didn't reach out to her.

Anna Murray Douglass was considered one of the first agents of the Underground Railroad and "an untiring worker along that line." Although Anna's increasing family and household duties prevented her educational advancement, Rosetta said her mother was able to read a basic letter, but Rosetta was instructed to read to her. Most likely, Rosetta would have read to her mother while Anna was binding shoes or doing other chores. Anna took a lively interest in all aspects of the antislavery movement. Anna was no different from competent adults of her time who would have had many skills but could not read much or at all.

Over the years, the Douglass family helped about five hundred slaves escape to Canada. It wasn't unusual for a sleigh full of a dozen runaways to arrive at their home in the dead of winter, especially over the holidays when supervision was looser and slaves were given passes to visit relatives on distant plantations. In her husband's absence, Anna called the boys to start fires in the part of the house where fugitive slaves were hidden.

Chapter 5
1860s

In March 1860, Charles Douglass, age fifteen, wrote to his father from Lockport, New York, and described a visit with a family that included five girls. He had helped feed the cows, ate supper and skated until 8:30 p.m., then sent a quick note before bed since he had to be up at 5:00 a.m.

While he was in England, Frederick Douglass was distraught over the news that his daughter Annie had died in March 1860, a few days before her eleventh birthday. Before her death, she had lost the power to speak or hear. He was convinced her death resulted from anxiety over his safety and deep sorrow over the death of John Brown, on whose knee she had so often sat.

Skaters on the Genesee River near the home of the Douglass family. *Rochester Images, Rochester Public Library Local History Division.*

Samuel D. Porter's family arranged for her burial in their lot in Mount Hope Cemetery later that month.

Despite fear for his safety, Douglass returned to Rochester. Cemetery records say Annie Douglass died of congestion of the brain. The Douglass family then bought their own family plot in July 1860.

Famous Rochester nurseryman George Ellwanger built a house on South Avenue near the Douglass homestead in 1861 and sold it in 1862 to a lawyer whose son-in-law was named Halsey. The Halsey House, also known as the Neun House or Mansion, is an undocumented stop on the Underground Railroad.

Anna Douglass was devastated by the death of their youngest child, daughter Annie. *Frederick Douglass National Park.*

Emancipation Proclamation

When President Lincoln signed the Emancipation Proclamation in September 1862, he declared freedom for all slaves in the Confederate States if those states did not return to the Union by January 1, 1863. That

The inscription for Annie Douglass is on the left side of the Douglass gravestone in Mount Hope Cemetery. *Robert P. Meadows.*

day marked the end of slavery in the Confederate States, but not in the border states of Delaware, Kentucky, Maryland, Missouri and West Virginia or any Southern state under Union control.

After the Emancipation Proclamation, Governor John Andrew of Massachusetts was authorized to raise a regiment of black volunteers.

A popular cartoon before the Civil War. *Rochester Images, Rochester Public Library Local History Division.*

Although Frederick Douglass regretted that New York State had not been the first to call for black soldiers, he wrote a stirring appeal, "Men of Color, To Arms," urging free black males to join the Fifty-fourth Massachusetts Volunteer Infantry. The Fifty-fourth was the vanguard of about 180,000 black troops who served; more than 4,000 belonged to regiments raised in New York State.

Many doubted they would fight, but Douglass claimed, "Once let the black man get upon his person the brass letters U.S., let him get an eagle on his button, and a musket on his shoulder and bullets in his pocket, and there is no power on earth which can deny that he has earned the right to citizenship in the United States." He helped enlist over one hundred men from upstate for the Fifty-fourth. For the rest of his life, Douglass looked upon the Emancipation Proclamation as the greatest turning point in American history and the most crucial event in African American history.

Charles Douglass was the first black man in Monroe County to enlist in the Massachusetts Fifty-fourth Regiment. After both his sons, Lewis and Charles, enlisted, Douglass proudly watched the Fifty-fourth Regiment leave Boston for the war in the South. He and other blacks soon realized that Negro troops were placed in segregated units under white officers and received less pay than white soldiers of similar rank. Worse, some captured soldiers were killed or sold into slavery.

Charles Douglass became ill, which was not uncommon, and didn't leave for the South, but Lewis helped lead the Fifty-fourth Massachusetts Regiment of black infantry in a brutal battle in July 1863 against Fort Wagner. During the attack on this artillery post on Morris Island that guarded Charleston Harbor (as shown in the 1989 movie *Glory*), 174 Confederate defenders were killed or wounded, and 1,515 Union soldiers fell. The Confederates helped bury the black soldiers in a common grave, including their aristocratic white leader, Colonel Robert Gould Shaw, whose death made him another saint for the North.

Lewis Douglass became sergeant major of the Fifty-fourth Massachusetts Regiment and was known as the "Lion of the Regiment." He survived the attack on Fort Wagner and described the night assault in Charleston Harbor in a letter to his father that was printed in the *Rochester Daily Democrat* on August 15, 1863.

Also that July 1863, Douglass met with both President Lincoln and his secretary of war, Edwin Stanton, to share his concern about the slow recruitment of black soldiers. In order to devote himself to recruiting, he wrote the last editorial for his newspaper and stopped publishing it in August 1863. When Stanton promised him a commission if he would aid in the recruitment of black soldiers, Douglass returned to Rochester with high expectations. The last issue of Douglass's paper was printed on August 16, 1863, but the promised commission never arrived.

In August 1863, the family learned that Lewis

Undated photo of Rosetta Douglass as a young woman. *Frederick Douglass National Park.*

75

Left: Granddaughter Annie Sprague was said to resemble her namesake, Annie Douglass, very much. *Frederick Douglass National Park.*

Below: Rochester has earned its reputation for unpredictable weather, as shown by this flood in 1865. *Rochester Images, Rochester Public Library Local History Division.*

Douglass was seriously ill and, after several difficult weeks, was in a military hospital in New York City. While Anna stayed in Rochester, Frederick, often with Ottilie Assing, went to see him daily for three weeks. Assing described Lewis as "an educated and pleasant young man."

In the midst of the chaos of the Civil War, Rosetta married Nathan Sprague in Rochester on December 24, 1863.

In October 1864, Charles wrote to his father that he "had a very fine time with Nathan at Elmira," whom he said would no doubt be staying there for the winter.

In February 1865, Rosetta wrote to her father, who was in Philadelphia, that Lewis was home and not as violently sick as he had been. She wrote that Nathan was in Hilton Head after having been switched frvom one regiment, in which he refused to serve, back to the Fifty-fourth, and the officers would be sending him to do duty in Savannah. She complained of being "so housed all winter I am glad of the chance to go to the office…Mother takes charge of little Annie. She grows more and more playful each day she lives. Mother sends love[,] also Lewis['] baby would send hers if she could speak."

From 1865 to 1872, Rosetta and Nathan Sprague moved in and out of the Douglass home in Rochester as Nathan struggled to support his family. (By 1872, he and Rosetta had five girls: Annie, Harriet, Alice, Estelle and Fredericka.)

RETURN TO MARYLAND

After slavery was abolished in Maryland in early November 1864, Frederick Douglass returned to Baltimore for the first time in twenty-six years. At the time, the Union had been saved, the war had been won, Lincoln had been reelected and the power of slavery in the South had been crushed. Douglass had left Baltimore as a frightened runaway and returned as a successful and famous advisor to the president. The audience at Douglass's first speech, an emancipation celebration at Bethel African Methodist Church in Fells Point, was integrated—something he would never have seen in his youth. The speech he gave that night was one of the most emotional of his life.

Frederick Douglass said after the South's surrender in 1865, "Slavery is not abolished until the black man has the ballot." (It took until 1872 for the Fifteenth Amendment to make this happen.)

According to the late Rochester author Henry Clune, "Frederick Douglass was a chattel waif who ran away from a Maryland slaveholder and rose to such eminence that President Lincoln called him one of the most meritorious men, if not the most meritorious man in the United States."

President Abraham Lincoln's wife, Mary Todd Lincoln, served as first lady from 1861 until her husband's assassination on April 14, 1865. Although she had a brother and three half-brothers in the Confederate army, she believed in freedom for all black men, women and children. She was a quiet but determined abolitionist who visited wounded soldiers and raised money for widows and orphans. She was the first first lady to invite black Americans to the White House as guests.

After President Lincoln was shot, Mary Lincoln sent Frederick Douglass her husband's favorite walking cane because Douglass collected them and she believed her husband would have wanted him to have it.

Years later, in a speech commemorating Abraham Lincoln's birthday, Douglass described how Mary Todd Lincoln used to tell abolitionists who were frustrated with her husband, "Oh, yes, Father is slow." He then told that when she was leaving the White House to return to Illinois, she said to her dressmaker, "Here is Mr. Lincoln's favorite cane (this is the identical cane that I now hold in my hand), and I know of no man who will value it more than Frederick Douglass." Mrs. Lincoln had it sent to him in Rochester, New York. "I am the owner of this cane, you may depend on that; and I mean to hold it and keep [it] in sacred remembrance of Abraham Lincoln, who once leaned upon it."

In August 1865, Douglass wrote to Mrs. Lincoln thanking her for the cane as "an indication of his humane interest in the welfare of my whole race."

FAMILY MATTERS

In February 1866, Charles, now twenty-one, wrote to his father, who was to speak in St. Louis, Missouri, that they'd had terrible weather in Rochester since he'd left and the thermometer was six above zero with snow drifted higher than the fences in some places while the ground was bare in others. The weather was so bad that the roads were buried in heaps of snow that didn't thaw because every few days they got another snowstorm. He also mentioned that Lewis was being paid seventy-five cents a week to teach about thirty students at night school and that if he could, he (Charles) would jump at the chance to buy farmland but couldn't afford to.

During the summer of 1866, Nathan Sprague joined his wife and daughter Annie at the Douglass home, where Rosetta had moved, as they were expecting

Undated photo of Charles Douglass as a young man. *Frederick Douglass National Park.*

another child and could not afford a house of their own. Charles also came back from the war with his wife, Mary Elizabeth Murphy, called Libbie, while Lewis and Fred Jr. had just left for work at the Red, White and Blue Mining Company in Colorado. During the summer of 1865, Charles had adopted a thirteen-year-old ex-slave, Henry Strothers of Georgia, whom he had sent to Rochester to

Undated image of young Frederick Douglass Jr.
Frederick Douglass National Park.

stay with the family. Charles wrote that Henry could milk, take care of horses and was used to most any kind of work. Invitations to the house were also extended to Ottilie Assing, who stayed there that summer.

In October 1866, Lewis, now twenty-six, wrote from Denver that since his laundry business failed, he and Fred had opened a lunchroom with the help of a businessman. It cost them $100, and after being open for two weeks, they had paid off half of their debt. He wrote, "In my business I am up early and late."

In March 1867, Nathan Sprague wrote, "I have let my farm go for a house and lot." He and Rosetta had moved into a house at 62 Pearl Street in Rochester, saying, "Annie is the only one that seems not to like her new home as she every little while cries to go home."

In her own letter, Rosetta regretted not living out on a piece of land where she could make her own butter but was relieved to live in the city without the debt of a farm "straining every nerve." She said there were three Quaker families to one side and two Irish families on the other and that Mother had come down one day to help her get "somewhat-put-to rights." She described Hamiel, their four-month-old daughter, as "very good and lively" and weighing sixteen pounds.

Later that April, when Nathan bought horses and a hack, they were doing well. Rosetta gave birth to her second child, a daughter named Harriet.

Charles wrote a letter to the family in Rochester, also in April, about his being the second colored man in the government to receive a first-class clerkship. In May, he wrote that he had received his first $100 for one month's service, that his board was $25 a month and that rents were very high in the city. Since the cheapest way to live was to get a small lot on the outskirts of the city, he hoped his father would help him with $1,000 to put down on a lot. In a later letter, Charles accepted his father's advice to wait to buy a lot until he was able to do so with his own earnings.

PAINFUL REUNION

In the summer of 1867, Frederick Douglass met his brother, Perry Downs, for the first time in forty years. Perry had survived fifty years of slavery, most in the Deep South after following his wife to Texas after she had been sold. Perry contacted Frederick and, with assistance, came to Rochester with his wife and four children. Frederick quickly had a small house built next to his own for them. Although Douglass was overjoyed at the reunion, seeing his uneducated, deeply scarred brother "was too affecting for words to describe."

Less than a year later, Perry and his family returned to the Eastern Shore of Maryland because they didn't like Rochester's cold winters. Their stay must have been awkward, for Charles wrote in August 1867, "From what I have heard of their conduct I should be afraid even to have them in the same neighborhood, and more especially when you are away in the winter months."

In 1867, Lewis and Frederick Jr. were working for a mining company in Denver—Lewis as secretary and Fred Jr. in the printing office. In the spring of 1867, Charles had been hired by the Freedmen's Bureau in Washington and went there quickly to earn $100 a month, leaving his pregnant wife, Libbie, with his mother.

In June 1868, Charles thanked his father for $500 toward purchasing two lots. He planned to fence them in and sow them with cabbage, which had sold for twenty cents a head over the winter in D.C. A week later, he asked to have a trunk, his new axe, books, dishes and

Charles wrote about his new baby and plans to sow cabbage. *Rochester Images, Rochester Public Library Local History Division.*

curtains sent to them, including items that would help Libbie make things for the baby. He said Freddie had five teeth and could almost talk, "ahead of all the babies around here."

The following week, Charles estimated it would cost him $300 for lumber and another $250 to get his house put up, which would take about six weeks. He told his father the Bureau of Refugees, Freedmen and Abandoned Lots was to be discontinued, but the Educational Department where he worked would continue. He also repeated, "Baby has five teeth and will soon talk."

Toward the end of July 1868, Charles wrote to his father that he had arranged to have someone buy lumber for him so he could repay it on a payment plan and start building his house. A short time later, in August, Charles wrote to him that work had started, but it had been raining for a week and there was plenty of mud. In September, Charles wrote to his father describing the house as being "20ft front by 38ft back" and having a roof and the sides closed in.

Charles said when the house was finished, it would have cost him $800 and be worth $1,200. He also mentioned applying for the position of superintendent of the new village, which paid $1,400 a year. Later that week, Charles wrote to thank his father for the extra $300; he also mentioned that his son was quite sick and that the summer had been hard on children there, with as many as seventeen dying in one day.

After Charles and Libbie moved into their house at the end of October 1868, he wrote to his father that Fred would do well in his store, which was nearly finished.

At the beginning of January 1869, Charles wished his father a long and prosperous life, mentioned that Libbie had been sick for a month and asked him if he would attend the National Colored Convention later in the month. He said that he was teaching night school at the house for about ten students at fifty cents per month, and once he had thirty or forty pupils, he could use the bureau's schoolhouse. Their boy was very fond of music and hummed a tune correctly.

Charles's letter at the beginning of September mentions Lewis being in good spirits over his upcoming wedding. Charles doubted he could afford the suit of clothes and travel money because he had a doctor's bill of forty-eight dollars to pay.

In 1869, Lewis Douglass married Amelia, the daughter of Jermain and Caroline Loguen, abolitionists from Syracuse, New York. Her father, Jermain Loguen, is said to have helped 1,500 runaways as "superintendent" of Syracuse's Underground Railroad station.

Lewis Douglass and Amelia Loguen were married in 1869. *Frederick Douglass National Park.*

Lewis and Fred Jr. became printers, with Lewis finding work in the Government Printing Office through his father's connections. Fred eventually became a writer and editor; Charles worked as a clerk in the Freedmen's Bureau of the Treasury Department and later as a consul for Santo Domingo.

Charles wrote a long, confidential letter to his father in June 1870. He had six hundred hills of sweet potatoes, and room for three hundred more, and so many strawberries that their suppers consisted mostly of them. He

CHARLES DOUGLASS may have played for the Unexpected, a local black club organized by Frank Stewart in 1866, which followed the rules and customs of the National Association from which it was excluded. Before the Civil War, baseball teams in Rochester and across America had been integrated but were not afterward.

In family news from 1872, Charles was constantly busy with the supervision of two school buildings that were being built. He had killed and smoked his hogs, over five hundred pounds' worth, and the weather was fine.

also complained that his father expected him to save, but that was hard to do with Lewis and Fred being out of work and staying with him for months, while he also lost his job and found another. The promotion he was expecting wasn't going to come through for several more months, and he used the money sent to buy clothes and boots for his brothers and had tried hard to shoulder their care, despite being the youngest. He mentioned having lost ten pounds and that he had stinging pains all through his left side from shoulder to hip, half a dozen times a day, that he attributed to "exposure during the war."

Then in August, Charles received his father's invitation to the members of the "Mutuals" to dine in Rochester during the baseball team's pending visit. Charles said there would be ten or eleven expected.

That September, the *Rochester Evening Express* noted that Frederick and Anna Douglass hosted the visiting black baseball team, the Washington, D.C. Mutuals. The team's roster included their son Charles, who had played on a Rochester team before joining the green-stockinged Mutuals.

THE FIFTEENTH AMENDMENT

After the Fifteenth Amendment granting black men the right to vote took effect in March 1870, the American Anti-Slavery Society met for the last time in April 1870. Speaking at the jubilant gathering of old friends, Frederick Douglass said, "I seem to find myself to be living in a new world."

Debate over the Fifteenth Amendment had stirred up controversy at the National Woman's Suffrage Association's convention in 1869 in Washington,

D.C. Elizabeth Cady Stanton considered it an open, deliberate insult to American womanhood.

The National Woman's Suffrage Association (NWSA), founded in 1869 and based in New York City, was begun by Susan B. Anthony and Elizabeth Cady Stanton when the women's rights movement split into two groups over the question of suffrage for African American men. Considered the more radical of the two, the NWSA aimed to secure the right to vote for women, and the group often stirred public debate through its reform proposals on social issues, including marriage and divorce.

(The NWSA invited all woman suffrage societies in the United States to become auxiliaries and grew considerably by the time it reunited with its sister organization, the American Woman Suffrage Association, in 1890.)

THE NATIONAL ERA

Frederick Douglass had bought another newspaper, the *National Era*, in 1870 to promote the rights of women and blacks and also considered running for public office. While Douglass claimed the mission of the *National Era* was the elevation of his race, he was also motivated to set up Lewis and Fred Jr. in business. They had returned East after their venture in Colorado failed.

Unfortunately, the government jobs their father found for them were shaky; due to federal budget cuts, Charles lost his in the spring of 1869. When Lewis found a job in the Government Printing Office, where he was called an untrained scab, he worked at lower wages than those denied him by exclusion from the Printer's Union.

Chapter 6
The Washington Years

Frederick Douglass was spending most of his time in Washington, D.C., so that when a suspicious fire in June 1872 destroyed the Douglass home on South Avenue, the family moved there.

The Douglass family lost over $4,000 in the fire that destroyed their South Avenue homestead. Among the losses was the only complete set of the *North Star*, the *Frederick Douglass Paper* and the *Douglass Monthly*. Shortly after the fire, Douglass was awarded an honorary law degree from Howard University at its first commencement. Then in July, the family moved to a house on A Street in Washington, D.C.

Six acres of the Douglass property in Rochester were sold to the Brueck family in 1872. The property was later sold to the Keller family and used as a nursery, which is on the City of Rochester plat map of 1875.

In the meantime, Rosetta and Nathan Sprague, who had seven children, lived in a house her father owned on Hamilton Place. Douglass deeded the house to her in 1872 and most likely stayed there whenever he was in town. The house was sold after Douglass's death in 1895. It can still be seen on the corner of Bond and Hamilton Streets, near South Clinton Avenue in southeast Rochester.

After her parents went to Washington, D.C., Rosetta Sprague said of their Rochester homestead, "Perhaps no other home received under its roof a more varied class of people than did our home. From the highest dignitaries to the lowliest person, bond or free, white or black were welcomed, and mother was equally gracious to all."

Frederick Douglass owned the house where his daughter and her family lived on Hamilton Place. *Robert P. Meadows.*

THE PRESIDENTIAL ELECTION OF 1872

Although Frederick Douglass was honored by being the first black nominated for vice president by the Equal Rights Party, he chose to win the black vote for President Grant's 1872 reelection campaign. He went to Washington with the expectation of a cabinet appointment or other office. Though he had considered moving there for some time, the loss of his home in Rochester forced the timing.

The crash of banking houses that began in September 1873 closed the New York Stock Exchange for ten days. Many American railroads, which had been overinvested, went bankrupt; unemployment was high; and a severe recession began that was followed by five years of depression.

In the spring of 1874, in the middle of this financial depression, when the Freedman's Saving and Trust Co. had a deficit of $200,000, the trustees offered Frederick Douglass the presidency to inspire confidence among black depositors and prevent its collapse. The dream lasted three months.

In June, Douglass secured an act from Congress placing the company in bankruptcy. Then, in September 1874, Douglass and his sons

DURING THE WINTER of 1871, Elizabeth Cady Stanton had written in support of prominent feminist and publisher Victoria Woodhull's lobbying efforts for women's rights in Washington, D.C. Stanton not only admired the *Woodhull and Claflin Weekly* but also Woodhull's independence and money. Woodhull went on a whistle-stop speaking tour, lecturing on "Social Freedom" the first night at Corinthian Hall in Rochester and then in Dunkirk, New York; Cleveland; Detroit; Toledo; Buffalo; and Erie, Pennsylvania. The *Rochester Evening Express* described her as a woman of remarkable originality and power and the ablest advocate of women's suffrage. Like Frederick Douglass, Victoria Woodhull had moved from poverty to fame.

In the spring of 1872, Woodhull organized a grand convention in Apollo Hall in New York for a new political party, the Equal Rights Party. Woodhull was nominated by the new party for the office of president of the United States. The party planned to announce its selection of Frederick Douglass as a running mate to match her representation of the oppressed sex with his of the oppressed race. However, Douglass was at a national convention in New Orleans, and due to a severe recession in which four thousand businesses failed in 1872, Woodhull's Equal Rights Party bonds didn't sell. Susan B. Anthony had not supported Woodhull's candidacy, but other suffragists did, and many of them planned to vote in the upcoming national election.

ROCHESTER RESIDENT and women's rights advocate Susan B. Anthony registered to vote on November 1, 1872. When she then voted in the presidential election in Rochester, she was arrested. Her trial began in June 1873 in Canandaigua, Ontario County, so she could have a more fair trial than in Rochester.

published the last issue of the *New National Era* at a personal loss of over $10,000. To make ends meet, he returned to the lecture circuit at a time when lectures were still a popular form of entertainment. He had not lost his ability to captivate audiences and spoke on a wide variety of topics, earning as much as $200 per speech.

By the Front Door

In June 1877, Douglass went back to St. Michaels, Maryland, after having been away for forty-one years. There he met with Thomas Auld, entering Auld's house by the front door as compared to the back. After an emotional greeting between the shrunken, dying elderly man in his bed and the tall, well-dressed Douglass, Frederick asked him how he had reacted to his escape. Auld said, "I always knew you were too smart to be a slave, and had I been in your place, I should have done as you did."

Newspaper accounts of Douglass's speech that afternoon expressed shock at his addressing a mixed-race group in a picnic grove. After boasting of

The Douglass family's home on A Street, in Washington, D.C. *Frederick Douglass National Park.*

being an "Eastern Shoreman," he startled the audience by saying that he did not believe colored people were in any way inferior to whites, but until they could do what white people did, they were.

That summer, the Douglass family lived in a house on A Street in Washington, where they added a wing for their extended family. In September, Rosetta, who had been put out on the street in Rochester by creditors, arrived with her children, while her husband, Nathan, went to launch a business as a baker in Omaha, Nebraska. Louisa, Nathan Sprague's sister, helped Anna with the household and nursed Anna, who was often sick. Charles, who had lost his job, and his wife, Libbie, who was very ill, stayed there, too.

At the end of August 1877, after a long and tedious passage of eleven days, Charles Douglass wrote his father a letter from Puerto Plata in the Dominican Republic. He described a political situation that had been unsettled by coups and counter-coups in the last year.

In 1877, Frederick Douglass finally got relief from pressure of the lecture circuit and long stretches away from home when President Rutherford B. Hayes appointed him United States marshal for the District of Columbia. Douglass was the first black man to serve in this position, holding the post from 1877 to 1881.

Frederick Douglass celebrated his financial stability in 1878 by buying Cedar Hill, an estate with a twenty-room Victorian house. It was in the village of Uniontown, surrounded by the Anacostia hills. In addition to the house, the property had a barn and large vegetable and flower gardens like those he and Anna had enjoyed in Rochester. It was set on nine acres, some wooded and some cleared for farms.

The following year, he bought fifteen adjacent acres. In 1879, he had three families to support in addition to his own: Rosetta and her children while Nathan was in Omaha; Charles, who was a widower, and his children; and his brother Perry and Perry's daughter. Perry was dying, and Douglass was glad to have shelter for him.

Ottilie Assing, who stayed at Cedar Hill from mid-September to December 1878, got caught up in the presidential election in which Douglass campaigned for Republican James Garfield. She enjoyed social life in Washington and was particularly pleased with a visit at Cedar Hill by Rutherford Hayes, who was welcomed by Frederick and Anna and herself.

Rosetta's oldest children, her sister-in-law Louisa and Charles's children also lived at Cedar Hill. Charles had found a job and was about to remarry. Douglass's brother Perry had died, but a half sister, Aunt Kitty, with her son

Cedar Hill, Frederick and Anna's home in Uniontown, in the District of Columbia. *Rochester Images, Rochester Public Library Local History Division.*

and his wife, soon moved in. There was also the eleven-year-old grandson of another half sister who had been orphaned.

In June 1879, a bust of Frederick Douglass that was unveiled in Sibley Hall at the University of Rochester was a sign of his immense popularity. He is considered the first Rochestarian to gain the distinction of national and international fame. When it was unveiled, Rochester's *Democrat and Chronicle* highly praised his character and accomplishments.

Even so, the *Rochester Democrat* reported that the unveiling ceremonies were "too informal," since Douglass hadn't been officially notified and learned about it privately (from his friend Samuel Porter).

In a stirring letter that was printed on July 2, 1879, Douglass said he was no longer amazed at such oversights but marveled at how far he had come. He recalled the times when he was a child fighting with his mother's dog for a few crumbs that fell from the table.

Frederick and Anna Douglass had twenty grandchildren from their four children who survived to adulthood. Out of the twenty, nine survived childhood. Pain over his daughter Annie's death lingered for the rest of his life, but it was lessened by the birth of Rosetta's daughter Annie, who looked like her namesake. In his later years, he became more of a family man than he had been able to be when his own children were growing up.

1880s

When President Garfield appointed Frederick Douglass as recorder of deeds for the District of Columbia, he served from 1881 until 1886. The post gave him money and prestige without any authority. Once Douglass started walking the five miles from Cedar Hill to his new office, his health improved.

Then, in 1882, he hired a new clerk, Helen Pitts (1838–1903), the daughter of Gideon and Jane Wills Pitts, abolitionists from Honeoye, a farming community in Ontario County, New York.

Helen had moved to Uniontown in 1880 to live with her uncle Hiram Pitts at his home, which was high on a slope next to Cedar Hill. Being single, she had to support herself, but having graduated from Mount Holyoke Seminary, it was unlikely she would find any work that matched her abilities. She worked in the pension office, but when she heard there was an opening in the recorder's office, she applied for it.

Helen Pitts was active in women's rights and collaborated with Caroline Winslow, president of the Moral Education Society of Washington, in publishing a radical feminist newspaper, the *Alpha*. Douglass and she first met as neighbors, although she may have had memories of meeting him as a girl because her father had met him in the 1840s. After she started working in his office, he found he could rely on her competency while he was away giving lectures. His third autobiography, *Life and Times of Frederick Douglass*, had come out in 1881 but was not as popular as his previous books. The public did not appreciate the message that the story of slavery should not be erased from the nation's memory.

In 1880 Helen Pitts moved to Uniontown, where she was a neighbor of the Douglass family. *Frederick Douglass National Park.*

Anna Murray Douglass, who suffered from chronic rheumatism, had a stroke in July 1882 and died in early August. Sometime after her death, Frederick, his daughter

Rosetta Sprague and his granddaughter Annie Sprague took the train to Rochester at Amy Post's invitation and stayed there.

Lewis told his father in a long letter in late July 1883 to stay away "from the heat and worry in Washington." Work in the office of the recorder of deeds was slow. Miss Pitts would be out of work the following day and another worker shortly. He and Amelia had visited at Cedar Hill the previous Sunday and found the cool breezes refreshing, and they were to go over and play croquet that afternoon.

The text for Anna Murray Douglass is on the right side of the Douglass family gravestone. *Robert P. Meadows.*

Fred Jr. also wrote in late July of his happiness at hearing from his father and that his health was improving. In response to criticisms aimed at Douglass, he said not to let himself to be troubled: "I think that with the truth on our side, Lew, Charley and I will be able to keep the flies off."

Rosetta wrote to him at the same time, saying that she was staying one night a week at Cedar Hill since he had been gone. "It is very quiet this evening[.] Rosa and Charlie are abed." She also worked in the recorder of deeds office with Helen Pitts and another woman.

During the summer of 1883, Frederick Douglass was severely depressed and apologized for declining an invitation to speak at the National Convention of Colored Men that September. He was further upset that October by the civil rights cases decision handed down by the Supreme Court, which voted eight to one that the owners of places of public accommodations were not required to admit black patrons.

Douglass considered breaking up the house but decided it was too late in life to change. Nathan Sprague's sister Louisa, who had been living there taking care of Anna, served as an informal housekeeper, with help from granddaughter Annie Sprague.

SECOND MARRIAGE

In January 1884, Frederick Douglass quietly applied for a marriage license at city hall in the District of Columbia. He and Helen Pitts drove to the parsonage of the Fifteenth Street Presbyterian Church, the home of Reverend Francis and Charlotte Forten Grimke. Not only was the church one of the nation's most distinguished African American churches, but Reverend Grimke was also one of the most well-known sons of an interracial union between a slave mother and an aristocratic South Carolinian father.

While neither Douglass's children nor Helen's family took the marriage well, Elizabeth Cady Stanton congratulated him and wished "that all the happiness possible in a true union be yours." Longtime friend Julia Griffiths Crofts also sent her most sincere congratulations.

When asked about his interracial marriage, Frederick answered that his first wife "was the color of my mother, and the second, the color of my father."

After the couple took an extended wedding trip to Chicago, Battle Creek, Niagara Falls, Rochester, Geneva, Syracuse, Oswego, Thousand Islands, Montreal, White Mountains, Portland, Boston, Fall River and New Bedford, he wrote to Amy Post that they traveled without receiving a single insult the whole way. He also thanked her for her congratulations and good wishes.

Frederick Douglass had given an interview to a reporter from the *Washington Post* at his home in Cedar Hill the day after the marriage. He said he didn't see why there should be any comment, since it "is certainly not an event of public moment." He was surprised the newspapers would share matters that "every man holds most dear and sacred, the affairs of the family." Douglass said he no longer had any political plans and only wished "to live quietly and peaceably." He ended the interview saying, "There is no division of races. God Almighty made but one race. I adopt the theory that in time the variety of races will be blended into one…You may say that Frederick Douglass considers himself a member of the one race which exists."

When asked about her marriage, Helen said, "Love came to me and I was not afraid to marry the man I loved because of his color."

Douglass expressed his gratitude to activists Ida B. Wells and Charlotte Forten Grimke, who were the only women of their race to defend his marriage.

Frederick and his new wife were among those "who traveled many miles to attend" the funeral services for Wendell Philips at the Hollis Street Unitarian

Church in Boston in early February 1884. In a speech given later that month in Washington, Douglass described Philips, saying:

The ties that bound me to Wendell Phillips were closer and stronger than ties between most men…He was among the first of those noble anti-slavery men in Massachusetts, who, more than five and forty years ago gave me a heart-felt welcome to a home of freedom and a life of usefulness. I went to his funeral as to that of one of my own household; as to that of a life-long friend, an affectionate brother, one to whom I was indebted for offices the highest and best a great man can bestow upon his humble brother…The grief that he was gone was subdued by a sense of gratitude that he had been spared so long.

At a time when criticism of interracial marriage was very strong, author Louisa May Alcott sat with the couple at the funeral service.

Later that year, Douglass learned that Ottilie Assing had taken her own life in Paris in August and bequeathed him her library and the interest from a trust fund of $13,000.

After Democrat Grover Cleveland won the presidential election in 1884, Douglass remained in office for a year but resigned, at Cleveland's request, in March 1886. Douglass defended President Cleveland, who had invited him and Helen to dine at the White House.

Before beginning an extensive trip through Europe in September 1886, Douglass drew up a will that valued his estate, without Cedar Hill, at $85,000.

That fall, Frederick and Helen traveled to England, where they visited Julia Griffiths Crofts. They spent two months in Paris and then toured France, Italy, Egypt and Greece.

In February 1888, Douglass gave an address entitled "Old Men Can Be as Bashful as Young Men" at a public celebration in honor of his birth, organized by the Bethel Literary and Historical Association at Metropolitan AME Zion Church in Washington.

The *Evening Star* reported that the church was filled with admirers of the "foremost man of the colored race." In his opening comments, Douglass asked them why they would celebrate his seventy-first birthday. He said that day

was taken from him long before he had the means of owning it. Birthdays belong to free institutions. We, at the South, never knew them. We were born at times—harvest times, watermelon times, and generally hard times. I never knew anything about the celebration of a birthday except Washington's birthday, and it seems a little strange to have mine celebrated…For many reasons it would have been more in accordance with my feelings to sit quietly and not offer a remark…I have a feeling of timidity for old men can be bashful as well as young men…This demonstration…means that you consider that I have been a faithful, inflexible, unflagging, and persistent worker in the cause of liberty and of the ELEVATION OF THE COLORED PEOPLE.

FAMILY UPDATES

Fred Jr. wrote to his father in June 1887 about being furloughed by the deputy recorder. It took several letters for him to reveal that he was let go because of his father's stand as a steadfast Republican against the incumbent Democrats.

Charles wrote from 315 A Street Northeast in May 1889 that he knew he was behind in his rent since borrowing $100 and that he had become behind since owing $70 every ten weeks for Joseph's tuition, board and washing in Boston. Despite being sick and having a broken leg, he remained committed to paying all his debts.

That August 1889, Charles wrote a long letter about his complicated relationship with Nathan, with whom he had fallen out because of Nathan's attitude toward Douglass. Charles hoped to be promoted and be able to stay in the smaller of two houses on A Street at twenty-five dollars a month.

1890s

In 1891, Frederick Douglass, now seventy-three, resigned his post as minister to Haiti. During the years when he had been a Republican officeholder, his fame and fortune reached new heights. At home, he was treated as the preeminent leader of black America; abroad, he was treated like a nobleman.

Frederick Douglass's longtime associate, the Reverend Thomas James, died in April 1891 at his Rochester home on Tremont Street. His remains were buried in Mount Hope Cemetery.

When a reporter from *The New York World* interviewed Frederick Douglass at Cedar Hill in July 1891, Douglass had been playing croquet on the lawn with

Helen and some friends. Pointing to his house and lands, he said:

> What can the world give me more than I already possess? I am blessed with a loving wife, who in every sense of the word is a helpmate, who enters into all my joys and sorrows. I have children whose every aim is to do me credit. I have friends loyal and true whose great delight seems to be to gather close around me. What more can I want?

HISTORICAL MARKER

Once known as "Douglass Row," the houses at 516–524 S. Dallas Street were constructed by Frederick Douglass in the 1890s, probably on the foundations of the old Strawberry Alley Methodist Church.

(Located at 524 South Dallas Street, Baltimore, Maryland)

In 1892, Frederick Douglass built rental housing for blacks in the Fells Point area of Baltimore. The complex, called Douglass Place, had five two-story row houses, called alley houses, built in the area where he lived in his younger days.

Also in 1892, Frederick Douglass Jr. died in late July after a lingering illness. The few letters he sent to his father were written in beautiful penmanship and expressed perceptive ideas. His colleagues and printers at the *National Leader*, a church journal in Baltimore, remembered him fondly.

Of all the Douglass children, Fred Jr. never had strong health. He hadn't enlisted in the army during the Civil War and had difficulty getting settled in life afterward. Frederick Jr. and his wife, Virginia, had already lost their own son and third child, Frederick, at age fourteen, as well as others as young children. After Virginia's death in 1890, Fred Jr. lost the ability to cope, and Rosetta was concerned about him. His orphaned son, Charley Paul, age eleven, was first placed under the guardianship of the family lawyer, but Charley kept running away. The lawyer removed himself as guardian, and Charley's Uncle Lewis had to step in.

Frederick Douglass revised his third autobiography, *Life and Times of Frederick Douglass*, in 1892 and, like a black Ben Franklin, presented his life story as a triumph over adversity and a model for black America.

In a September 1892 interview with T. Thomas Fortune, editor of the *New York Age*, Fortune gave Douglass's answer to a question that he had asked in an earlier visit to Cedar Hills: Who are your favorite authors? The answer was: poets, William Shakespeare, Lord Byron, Robert Burns, William Cullen Bryant, John Greenleaf Whittier and Henry Wadsworth Longfellow; prose,

Frederick Douglass Jr. died in July 1892. *Rochester Images, Rochester Public Library Local History Division.*

Victor Hugo, Sir Walter Scott, Charlotte Bronte, Alexander Dumas and Theodore Weld. He considered a three-volume French edition of *The Count of Monte Cristo* among his prized possessions.

Douglass also mentioned being close to his grandson Joseph H. Douglass, who had studied at the New England Conservatory in Boston and taught at Howard University. Joseph was a virtuoso violinist who performed at the White House and was the first black artist to make a phonographic record.

Frederick Douglass, who had been surrounded by family struggles and political disappointments, had agreed to serve as Haiti's commissioner to the

Lewis Douglass in 1893. *Rochester Images, Rochester Public Library Local History Division.*

World's Columbian Exposition in Chicago. Douglass felt highly honored as the only African American to have an official role at the World's Fair. Not even a black guide or guard was appointed by the organizers.

In October 1892, he and Helen attended the fair's opening ceremonies and stayed in Chicago for the dedication of the Haitian pavilion. The event was so thoroughly segregated that black activist Ida Wells condemned it in a publication, *The Reason Why the Colored American Is Not in the World's Columbian Exposition*, which Douglass helped sponsor.

Charles wrote to his father in May 1893 about his new venture in the development of a parcel of land that was subdivided into lots of 50 by 150 feet. Some bordered Black Walnut Creek in a development he was calling Highland Beach. He had cleaned out the underbrush and was laying out the streets, which were to be named after prominent colored men "so far as there were streets enough to go around." Charles was also very concerned about his father's serious cough, which "has thrown stronger and younger men than you."

Rosetta wrote her father a short note in November 1893 that she was "utterly dazed and crushed" by the news of her daughter Annie's death. A few weeks later, Rosetta wrote to her father on Annie's birthday when Annie would have been twenty-seven. She said all the girls had come home and that Estelle had returned to Gloucester; Fredericka to Richardville, Virginia; and Hattie was to leave that week. She felt "unboundly grateful" for the loan of the monies.

Frederick Douglass still spoke publicly and in 1894 gave one of his last great lectures, "The Lesson of the Hour: Why the Negro Is Lynched." He condemned the press and much of the public for calling southern violence against blacks the "Negro Problem," saying it was the "old trick of misnaming things…There is nothing the matter with the Negro, whatever. He is all right.

Charles Douglass in 1893. *Rochester Images, Rochester Public Library Local History Division.*

Rosetta Douglass Sprague. *Frederick Douglass National Park.*

Learned or ignorant, he is all right. He is neither a lyncher, a mobocrat or an anarchist. He is now what he has ever been, a loyal, law-abiding, hard working and peaceable man." By calling injustice to blacks the Negro Problem, "one removes the burden of proof from the old master class and imposes it on the Negro."

President Benjamin Harrison had made Douglass minister and consul to Haiti in 1889. Some believed it was a way of getting him out of the way in Washington; others thought he had more important work to do at home than there, but Frederick considered it an honor he couldn't decline. While he did his best to serve his own country's interests, he found himself at odds with the Haitian people's needs. After the American press kept giving him unfavorable coverage, he resigned.

In reference to his role as minister to obtain a naval station for the United States there, Douglass wrote a long article that appeared in the *North American Review* in September and October 1891. He wrote:

Prejudice sets all logic at defiance. It takes no account of reason or consistency...

The attempt has been made to prove me indifferent to the acquisition of a naval station in Haiti…The fact is, that when some of these writers were in their petticoats, I have comprehended the value of such an acquisition, both in respect to American commerce and to American influence. The policy of obtaining such a station is not new…

DOUGLASS'S DEATH

On February 20, 1895, Douglass attended a women's rights rally in Washington, D.C., where he was publicly greeted by Susan B. Anthony. Later, at Cedar Hill, while waiting for a carriage and retelling the events of the day, he sank to his knees before he fell to the floor and died. He was seventy-seven years old.

His body lay in state at the Metropolitan African Methodist Episcopal Church in Washington, where hundreds of mourners came to pay their respects.

His funeral then took place in Rochester, where the procession of viewers lasted for five hours at Rochester's City Hall before removal to Central Presbyterian Church. Thousands joined the procession to Mount Hope Cemetery.

At a time when newspapers ran few photos, Rochester's *Union and Advertiser* printed a half dozen views of the funeral and places Frederick Douglass had known in Rochester in honor of the occasion.

When Elizabeth Cady Stanton read about Douglass's death in the newspaper, she wrote in her diary her memory of the first time she heard him speak at an antislavery rally in Boston: "Around him sat the greatest anti-slavery orators of the day, earnestly watching the effect of his eloquence on that immense audience, that laughed and wept by turns, completely carried away by the wondrous gifts of his pathos and humor."

Mount Hope, the first municipal Victorian cemetery in the United States, which was dedicated in 1838, has the distinction of being an unsegregated cemetery. Frederick Douglass was buried there because he had once said of Rochester, "I shall always feel more at home there than anywhere else in the country."

His remains were placed next to his daughter Annie and wife, Anna. Frederick and Anna's daughter Rosetta said, "Together they rest side by side and most befittingly within sight of the dear old home of hallowed memories and from which the panting fugitive, the weary traveler, the lonely emigrant of every clime, received food and shelter."

The funeral service at Central Presbyterian Church in Rochester. *Rochester Images, Rochester Public Library Local History Division.*

This marker is at the beginning of the path to the Douglass family plot in Mount Hope Cemetery, Rochester, New York. *Robert P. Meadows.*

This marker is at the start of the path to the Anthony family plot, also in Mount Hope Cemetery. *Robert P. Meadows.*

After his death, Helen Pitts Douglass wrote that she had received "accurate testimony" that made Frederick one year younger than his accepted age. His family had celebrated his birthday based on the sentiment that on his mother's last visit with him, she had called him her "Valentine" and given him a heart-shaped ginger cake. He decided later it might have been a birthday visit.

Near the Douglass family plot in Mount Hope Cemetery is the Anthony family plot and the marker for Susan B. Anthony, his good friend, who argued publicly with him whether blacks or women needed the vote most. Privately they had agreed: everyone did.

In 1896, the year after her father's death, Rosetta Douglass Sprague, who was a public speaker and lecturer, joined Harriet Tubman and Ida Wells-Barnett in founding the National Association of Colored Women.

PUBLIC MONUMENT

The Frederick Douglass Monument was unveiled in 1899 near the railroad station at Central Avenue and St. Paul Street in Rochester, New York. *Albert Stone Photo Collection, Rochester Museum & Science Center.*

Frederick Douglass had remarked at the unveiling of the Lincoln Civil War statue in Rochester's Washington Park in 1892 that African American soldiers were not represented. A project for a public monument had begun in 1895, when Rochester African American leader John W. Thompson began raising money for a memorial to African American Civil War soldiers. After Douglass's death, the monument committee decided to fund a statue of him instead, for which the government of Haiti made a large contribution.

The statue of Frederick Douglass was the first public monument to an African American in the country. It was created by sculptor Sydney W. Edwards, who used Douglass's son Charles as the model.

The dedication was held in downtown Rochester in June 1899. New York State governor Theodore "Teddy" Roosevelt, Helen Pitts Douglass and many prominent visitors attended the dedication on North St. Paul Street across from the railroad station.

Frederick Douglass had been a powerful, eloquent orator, author, newspaper editor and statesman who was the most famous black man of the 1800s and that century's most prominent black intellectual. His twenty-five years in Rochester, from 1847 to 1872, are considered the most productive of his life.

Chapter 7

1900 and Beyond

After his death, Frederick Douglass's children had wanted to sell Cedar Hill and divide the money, but Helen P. Douglass wanted to turn it into a memorial. In 1900, Helen borrowed money, bought the house and established the Frederick Douglass Memorial and Historical Association. She toured the country lecturing and raising money for the association until the last year of her life.

Although her wish was to be buried at Cedar Hill, laws prevented it. After her death in 1903 at age sixty-five, there was no funeral service, and she was quietly buried next to Frederick, Annie and Anna in Mount Hope Cemetery in Rochester, New York.

In a paper given at the Woman's Christian Temperance Union on May 10, 1900, Rosetta Douglass Sprague wrote, "The story of Frederick Douglass' hope and aspirations and longing desire for freedom has been told—you all know it. It was a story made possible through the unswerving loyalty of Anna Murray, to whose memory this paper is written." Among her recollections, Rosetta described her mother's crucial role as an untiring worker on the Underground Railroad, her sternness as a parent and her ability to read a letter. Rosetta Douglass Sprague died in 1906 and was buried in Mount Hope Cemetery, near some of her children.

In February 1923, Fredericka Douglass Sprague Perry reprinted her mother's address of May 10, 1900, "My Mother as I Recall Her." Fredericka dedicated it to the Noble Women of the National Association of Colored Women.

This view of the Douglass family plot shows Helen P. Douglass's tombstone, to the left of the larger one for Frederick Douglass. *Robert P. Meadows.*

Frederick and Anna Douglass's children were: Rosetta (1839–1906), Lewis Henry (1840–1908), Frederick Jr. (1842–1892), Charles Remond (1844–1920) and Anna (1849–1860).

The Douglass memorial statue was moved to Highland Park Bowl on South Avenue, within walking distance of the family's former home to the north and east of Mount Hope Cemetery. It was rededicated by Eureka Masonic Lodge 36 in September 1941. There are several inscription plaques on its base:

> *The best defense of free American Institutions is the heart of the American people themselves.*

> *One with God is a majority.*

> *I know of no rights of race superior to the rights of humanity.*

Starting in 1916, the National Association of Colored Women's Clubs helped keep Cedar Hill open to the public. The National Park Service bought Cedar

There are three notable quotations by F. Douglass on the plaque at the base of the statue, which was moved to Highland Park and rededicated in September 1941. *Robert P. Meadows.*

"THE BEST DEFENCE OF FREE AMERICAN INSTITUTIONS IS THE HEARTS OF THE AMERICAN PEOPLE THEMSELVES"

"ONE WITH GOD IS A MAJORITY"

"I KNOW OF NO RIGHTS OF RACE SUPERIOR TO THE RIGHTS OF HUMANITY"

Hill in 1962, including the collection of five thousand letters, pamphlets, books, speeches and other documents. These items were transferred to the Library of Congress ten years later and inventoried and microfilmed for public use.

The Douglass home at Cedar Hill includes a reproduction of Douglass's "Growlery"—a small outbuilding with a stove, bed and desk where he could work and "growl" when he was in a mood.

The Library of Congress owns the largest single collection of Douglass's correspondence. It was scanned and placed on the Internet as part of the National Digital Library Program in 1994 and includes seventy-four thousand items, among them photos, newspaper clippings, speech manuscripts, diaries, wills and three thousand letters to and from Douglass.

Some of his surviving correspondence is also in the National Archives and the Women's Rights National Historical Park in Seneca Falls, New York.

Rochester's Freedom Trail Commission, in collaboration with the Landmark Society of Western New York, placed a large marker on South Avenue at the site of the Douglass family home in February 2005.

In 2001, international artist Pepsy Kettavong created a larger-than-life sculpture in the Madison Street neighborhood where Susan B. Anthony had lived with her sister Mary. It was called *Let's Have Tea.*

This large marker was placed in front of the James P. Duffy No. 12 School, at 999 South Avenue, in February 2005 by the Freedom Trail Commission and the Landmark Society of Western New York. *Robert P. Meadows.*

This City of Rochester marker is at the site of the Douglass homestead at 999 South Avenue. *Robert P. Meadows.*

In 2001, Artist Pepsy Kettavong created this statue *Let's Have Tea* in the square near the house where Susan and Mary Anthony lived. *Rochester Images, Rochester City Hall Photo Lab.*

Left: Sisters Susan and Mary Anthony. *Rochester Images, Rochester Public Library Local History Division.*

Below: The new Frederick Douglass–Susan B. Anthony Bridge was dedicated on July 13, 2007. *Rochester Images, Rochester City Hall Photo Collection.*

Douglass Place in Fells Point, Baltimore, was listed on the National Register of Historic Places in 1983 and as part of the Maryland Historical Trust in 2008.

The City of Rochester replaced the fifty-year-old Troup Howell Bridge over the Genesee River in July 2007 with a new bridge named the Frederick Douglass–Susan B. Anthony Bridge.

Genealogy

Frederick Augustus Bailey Douglass: b. c. 1818, d. 1895.

Anna Murray Douglass: b. c. 1818, d. 1882.
1. Rosetta Douglass (1839–1906) married Nathan Sprague, b. MD c. 1841
Frederick Douglass's seven grandchildren: the Spragues
Annie Rosine Sprague Norris: b. 1865; d. 1893
Harriet Bailey Sprague: b. 1866; marker in Mt. Hope for Hattie says d. 11/1/1940
Alice Louise Sprague: buried 6/10/1875, age 6 dropsy of the heart; residence, Hamilton Pl.
Estelle Irene Sprague Weaver: b. 1869
Fredericka Douglass Sprague Perry: b. 1872
Herbert Douglass Sprague: b. 1875
Rosebelle Mary Sprague Jones: b. 1877

2. Lewis Henry Douglass (1840–1908) married Helen Amelia Loguen
No Children

3. Frederick Douglass Jr. (1842 –1892) married Virginia Hewlett
Frederick Douglass's seven grandchildren: the Douglasses
Frederick Aaron Douglass: b. 1871
Jean Hewlett Douglass
Lewis Henry Douglass

Maud Ardelle Douglass

Charles Paul Douglass

Gertrude Paul Douglass (Gertrude May Douglass buried in Mt. Hope, 5/22/1889; age 10).

Robert Small Douglass

4. Charles Remond Douglass (1844–1920)

A. married Mary Elizabeth Murphy, b. 1845.

Frederick Douglass's six grandchildren:

Charles Frederick Douglass: b. 1868, Mass.

Joseph Henry Douglass: b. 7.1868.

Annie Elizabeth Douglass (Eliza? c. 1855)

Julia Ada Douglass

Mary Louise Douglass

Edward Douglass

Frederick Douglass's one grandchild:

Haley George Douglass: b. 11.1881, NY.

5. Annie Douglass (1849–1860), buried 3/16/1860 in Mt. Hope

Frederick Douglass married Helen Pitts (second wife); they had no children. She died 12/7/1903, mitral regurgitation, Washington, D.C.

Frederick Douglass's Siblings:

Perry (1813–1878)

Sarah (1814–c. 1883)

Eliza (1816–after 1870)

Himself (1818–1895)

Kitty (1820–after 1849)

Arianna, (1822–after 1849)

Harriet (b. c. 1825).

1850 census: Rochester, Ward 7: Frederick, editor, age 33; Anna, 35; Rosetta, 11; Lewis Henry, 10; Fred. Jr. 8; Charles, 5; Annie 1; Charlotte Murray, 30, b. c. 1820, MD; Julia Griffiths, 32, b. c. 1818, Scotland. Value: $6,000.

1860 census: Rochester Ward 12, Frederick Douglass, 43, F. D. Paper; Anna, 43; Rosetta, 21; Louis, 20, printer; Fred, 19, printer; Charles, 16, printer. Also at this address: Richard Lorenz, age 50, b. 1810, England; Mary Ann Lorenz, age 21, b. c. 1831, England; John, age 12; George, 10, Sarah, 6, Charles, 2.

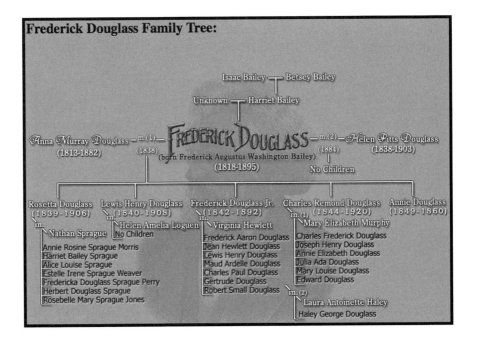

Frederick Douglass Family Tree:

Isaac Bailey — Betsey Bailey

Unknown — Harriet Bailey

Anna Murray Douglass — m.(1) — FREDERICK DOUGLASS — m.(2) — Helen Pitts Douglass
(1813-1882)   (1838)   (born Frederick Augustus Washington Bailey)   (1884)   (1838-1903)
                                (1818-1895)   No Children

Rosetta Douglass   Lewis Henry Douglass   Frederick Douglass Jr.   Charles Remond Douglass   Annie Douglass
(1839-1906)   (1840-1908)   (1842-1892)   (1844-1920)   (1849-1860)
m.   m.   m.   m.(1)
Nathan Sprague   Helen Amelia Loguen   Virginia Hewlett   Mary Elizabeth Murphy
                No Children

Annie Rosine Sprague Morris   Frederick Aaron Douglass   Charles Frederick Douglass
Harriet Bailey Sprague   Jean Hewlett Douglass   Joseph Henry Douglass
Alice Louise Sprague   Lewis Henry Douglass   Annie Elizabeth Douglass
Estelle Irene Sprague Weaver   Maud Ardelle Douglass   Julia Ada Douglass
Fredericka Douglass Sprague Perry   Charles Paul Douglass   Mary Louise Douglass
Herbert Douglass Sprague   Gertrude Douglass   Edward Douglass
Rosebelle Mary Sprague Jones   Robert Small Douglass
                            m.(2)
                            Laura Antoinette Haley
                            Haley George Douglass

1870 census: Nathan, gardener, Harriet, 4; Anna, 5; Allie, 1; Louise, 19 (most likely his sister), Ellen Louise, b. 1852, d. 1894.

1870 census: East of 7 St., Wash. D.C.: Charles R, 25, b. Mass.; Mary Elizabeth Murphy, wife, age 22, housewife. b. 10.1845; Charles F., 3, b. c.1867, NY; Jos. H, 1, b. c 1869, D.C.; Fred. D. Jr., 28, clerk, Treasury Dept., b. 1842, Mass.

House next door: Douglass, Elizabeth, 30, washerwoman, $300, b. c. 1840, MD; Elizabeth, 6; Theresa, 4; Eliza, 15, b. PA.

1880 census: Joseph H, age 10, b. c. 1870, Wash. D.C., at school, is listed under Fred. Jr.

1900 census: Charles F. Douglass, b. 1868, Mass., clerk in Gov't. Dept.; Joseph H., b. 7.1868, musician; b. 1881, married Laura Antoinette Haley aka Louisa, b. 7.1854, NY.

1880 census: on Nichols Ave., D.C.: Frederick, bailiff; Fred. A, 9; Charles F., (may be nephew) age 12, b. D.C.

1880 census: Nathan, farmer; Rosetta, 41; Annie, 15; Harriet, 14; Estelle, 10; Frederika, 8, Herbert, 5, Rosebelle, 3; and Marie Pongee, servant.

1900 census: Rosetta, b. June 1839; Hattie, b. Nov. 1868, teacher; Frederika, b. Aug. 1872, teacher; Rosebelle, Sept. 1877, teacher. [1900 census lists Haley George as a student and Joseph Henry as a musician.]

1910 census: lists Louisa Antoinette Haley as married for 29 years.

Bibliography

American Civil War. thelatinlibrary.com/chron/civilwar.html.

Astifan, Priscilla. "Baseball in the 19th Century. Part Two." *Rochester History* 62, no. 2 (Spring 2000).

———. "The Dawn of Professionalism." *Rochester History* 63, no. 1 (Winter 2001).

Beale, Irene. *Genesee Valley Women, 1743–1985.* Geneseo, NY: Chestnut Hill Press, 1985.

Bradford, Sarah. *Scenes from the Life of Harriet Tubman.* Auburn, 1869.

Burchard, Peter. *Frederick Douglass, For the Great Family of Man.* New York: Athenaeum, 2003.

"Charles R. Douglass." Rochester Photo Images, www.libraryweb.org.

Clune, Henry. *The Rochester I Know.* Garden City, NY: Doubleday, 1972.

Coles, Howard. *The Cradle of Freedom, A History of the Negro in Rochester, Western New York and Canada.* Vol. 1. N.p., 1941.

Cooley, Austin, and Vivian Cooley, owners of the Hallock House. Interview December 9, 2008.

Cooper, Mark Anthony, ed. *Dear Father, A Collection of Letters to Frederick Douglass from His Children, 1859–1894.* Philadelphia: Fulmore Press, 1990.

Cox, Clinton. *Fiery Vision.* New York: Scholastic Press, 1997.

Diedrich, Maria. *Love Across Color Lines.* New York: Hill and Wang, 1999.

Douglass Family Tree. http://international.loc.gov/ammem/doughtml/famtreet.html.

Douglass, Frederick. "Did John Brown Fail?" Speech at Harpers Ferry, West Virginia, May 30, 1881. In *Frederick Douglass Papers*, Series 1, Vol. 5, 1881–95, *Speeches, Debates, and Interviews.* Edited by John Blassingame and John McKivigan. New Haven, CT: Yale University Press, 1992.

———. *Douglass Autobiographies.* With notes by Henry Louis Gates. New York: Literary Classics of the United States, Inc. 1994.

———. Editorial. *Frederick Douglass Paper,* June 26, 1851.

———. Editorial. *North Star,* March 9, 1849. Available online at www.accessible.com.ezp.lib.rochester.edu.

———. *The Frederick Douglass Papers, Autobiographical Writings.* Series 2, Vol. 1, 1842–1852, *Narrative.* Edited by John Blassingame, John McKivigan and Peter Hanks. New Haven, CT: Yale University Press, 1999.

———. *The Frederick Douglass Papers.* Series 3, Vol. 1, *Correspondence.* Edited by John McKivigan. New Haven, CT: Yale University Press, 2009.

———. *Narrative of the Life of Frederick Douglass.* Introduction and notes by Robert O'Meally. New York: Barnes & Noble Classics, 2003.

———. *Narrative of the Life of Frederick Douglass.* Notes by John Chua. Lincoln, NE: Cliff Notes, 1996.

———. *Narrative of the Life of Frederick Douglass, An American Slave: Written by Himself.* Edited by Benjamin Quarles. Cambridge, MA: Belknap Press of Harvard University Press, 1960.

Du Bois, Eugene. *The City of Frederick Douglass.* Rochester, NY: Landmark Society of Western New York, 1994.

Du Bois, W.E.B. *John Brown.* New York: International Publishers, 1974.

Encyclopedia Brittanica, s.v. "*National Women's Rights Association.*" www.britannica.com.

Foner, Philip. *Frederick Douglass: Selected Speeches and Writings.* Abridged. Chicago: Lawrence Hill, 1999.

———. *Life and Writings of Frederick Douglass.* New York: International Publishers, 1950.

Frederick Douglass. N.p.: American Crisis Biographies, 1906.

Frederick Douglass National Historic Site: http://www.nps.gov/frdo/historyculture/Frederick-Douglass-Chronology.htm.

Gregory, James. *Frederick Douglass the Orator.* Springfield, MA: Willey Company, 1893.

Hallock, Bessie. "Here on This Hilltop." Typed family history, April 1962. Owned by A. and V. Cooley, 2008.

Hare, Mark. "Quakers Founded in 1650s." *Rochester Democrat & Chronicle,* November 17, 2008, 10A.

Historical Marker Database. "Born on Tuckahoe Creek." Historical Marker Database. Hmdb.org.

Hosmer, Howard. *Monroe County, 1821–1971.* Rochester, NY: Rochester Museum & Science Center, Flower City Printing, 1971.

Huggins, Nathan. *Slave and Citizen: The Life of Frederick Douglass.* N.p.: Library of American Biography Series, 1980.

Husted, Shirley Cox. *Sweet Gift of Freedom*: *Beyond the Battlefield*. Vol. 2. Rochester, NY: Monroe County Historian's Office, 1994.

Jacobs, Harriet. *Incidents in the Life of a Slave Girl, Written by Herself*. Edited by Jean Fagan Yellin. Cambridge, MA: Harvard College, 1987.

James, Thomas. "Autobiography of Rev. Thomas James." *Rochester History* 37, no. 4 (October 1975).

Klees, Emerson. *The Erie Canal in the Finger Lakes Region*. Rochester, NY: Friends of the Finger Lakes, 1996.

Kling, Warren. *America's First Boomtown: Rochester, NY: The Early Years and the Notables Who Shaped It*. Rochester, NY: Rochester History Alive Publications, 2008.

Lutz, Alma. "Susan B. Anthony and John Brown." *Rochester History* 15, no. 3 (July 1953).

Marcotte, Bob. "Anthony Steers Suffrage." *Rochester Democrat and Chronicle*, August 25, 2008.

———. "Black Regiment Proved Critics Wrong." *Rochester Democrat and Chronicle*, June 16, 2008.

McFeely, William. *Frederick Douglass*. New York: Norton, 1991.

McGowan, James. *Station Master on the Underground Railroad, Life and Letters of Thomas Garrett*. Moylan, PA: Whimsie Press, 1977.

McKelvey, Blake. "Lights and Shadows." *Rochester History* 21, no. 4 (October 1959).

———. *Rochester: A Brief History*. Lewiston, NY: Edwin Mellen Press, 1984.

———. "Rochester's Public Schools," *Rochester History* 31, no. 2 (April 1969).

McKelvey, Blake, and Ruth Rosenberg Naparsteck. *Rochester, A Panoramic History*. Sun Valley, CA: American Historical Press, 2001.

Miller, Douglass. *Frederick Douglass and the Fight for Freedom*. New York: Facts on File Pub., 1988.

National Historical Park. *Women's Rights*. Seneca Falls, NY: U.S. Dept. of the Interior, 1985.

National Parks. *Underground Railroad*. National Parks Service. www.nps.gov./history/nr/travel/underground/themee.htm National Parks.

Parker, Jane Marsh. *Letter*, April 6,1895.

Preston, Dickson. *The Young Frederick Douglass, The Maryland Years*. Baltimore, MD: Johns Hopkins University Press, 1980.

Quarles, Benjamin. *Frederick Douglass*. New York: Athenaeum, 1976.

———. Letter to Robert Kinnicut, October 9, 1859. Schomberg Collection.

———. *Narrative of the Life of Frederick Douglass*. Washington, D.C.: Associated Publishers, 1948.

Rochester Board of Education. *History of Public Schools of Rochester, 1813–1935*. Rochester, NY, 1935.

Rochester Democrat. "Frederick Douglass: Some of the Extraordinary Changes He Has Experienced." June 27, 1879.

"Rochester Population, 1812–1990," www. history.rochester.edu/canal/rochpop.htm.

Rosenberg-Naparsteck, Ruth. "A Growing Agitation." *Rochester History* 42, nos. 1&2 (January & April 1984).

Schmitt, Victoria. "Rochester's Frederick Douglass." Part 2. *Rochester History* 67, no. 4 (Fall 2005).

Sernett, Milton. *North Star Country*. Syracuse, NY: Syracuse University Press: 2002.

Skarmeas, Nancy. *First Ladies of the White House*. N.p.: Ideals Publications, 1995.

Sprague, Rosetta Douglass. "My Mother as I Recall Her." Reprinted February 14, 1923. Howard Coles archive, Schuyler Towsen Library, Rochester Museum and Science Center.

Susan B. Anthony House, Rochester, New York. "Information Sheet," ca. 2010.

Underhill, Lois Beachy. *The Woman Who Ran for President*. Bridgehampton, NY: Bridge Works, 1995.

Wagner, Sally Roesch. *Sisters in Spirit*. Summertown, TN: Native Voices, 2001.

Walvoord, Linda. *Rosetta, Rosetta, Sit by Me*. New York: Marshall Cavendish, 2004.

Weidt, Maryanne. *Voice of Freedom*. Minneapolis, MN: Carolrhoda Books, 2001.

Index

About the Author

R ose O'Keefe grew up in the suburbs of New York City, except for four years spent with her family living outside of Paris, France. After graduating from SUNY Potsdam during the Vietnam years, Rose moved to Rochester, New York, and discovered the beauty of the Genesee River Valley and Finger Lakes region on camping outings with family and friends. (She laughs now when people call Albany "Upstate.")

Since then, she has become a local historian with a special interest in the Frederick Douglass family's years in Rochester from 1847 to 1872. She has enjoyed sharing the history of Rochester's South Wedge, the southeast side of the city, and a broader look at history of the Greater Genesee Valley. This book reflects years of researching the Douglass family and its ties to Rochester, New York.